SHADOW
LIGHT
WORKBOOK

RECORDING YOUR SHADOW JOURNEY

SHADOW LIGHT WORKBOOK

RECORDING YOUR SHADOW JOURNEY

KEITH WITT

Copyright 2017 Integral Publishers
SHADOW LIGHT WORKBOOK: Recording Your Shadow Journey

Keith Witt
Integral Publishers
4845 E. 2nd Street
Tucson, AZ 85711
831-333-9200
ISBN: 978-1-4951-8777-3

Cover Design by QT Punque and Kathryn Lloyd
Interior Design by Kathryn Lloyd

Integral Coaching®, Integral Coach™, Integral Master Coach™,
and AQAL Constellation™ are registered trademarks in Canada of Integral
Coaching Canada Inc. and licensed to the authors.

To Becky, my life partner and best teacher.

TABLE OF CONTENTS

INTRODUCTION

Welcome to *The Shadow Light Workbook!*

After Integral Publishers and I put out *Shadow Light,* two of my editors, Russ Volckmann and Jeannie Carlisle, suggested we needed a workbook that organized the exercises from each chapter into a coherent framework of embodied practices.

It seemed like a great idea to me, and that's where *The Shadow Light Workbook* originated.

Practices are super important because of how we learn. Our right hemisphere is dominant for non-linear thought, morality, self-reflection, empathy, autobiographical narratives, habits, emotionally charged and relational language, and an integrated map of the body. Our left hemisphere is dominant for conscious deliberation, linear rational thought, language, and consciously learning new facts and routines.

We can learn a new routine in minutes or even seconds. For instance, focus for a few seconds on being aware with loving acceptance and caring intent of what you are feeling in your body. Got it? How does it feel? I always enjoy focusing on sensation and emotions with acceptance and caring intent.

If we want to make a new routine (like awareness of sensation/emotion with acceptance and caring intent) an enduring habit, we usually need to consciously repeat it many times—sometimes *thousands* of times. This is why regular practices are priceless. We can determine states and processes we want to naturally embody and *consciously* practice them regularly. This activates left hemisphere based superpowers of focused intent and action, in service of principle, and driven by resolve. At some point we don't need to decide *to do* the practices, because we *have become* the practices. Our constructive Shadow now offers them effortlessly and regularly.

Principles and ideas that light us up over time show up as new habits of being, relating, and acting—reflecting our maturing Shadow selves. If these new habits are of more compassion for wider ranges of beings and deeper consciousness and understanding of ourselves and others, our worldviews expand and change—a reflection of what we call vertical health in the Integral system.

I've included some introductory explanations for each practice. If you want to dive deeper, you can join me in the corresponding chapter of *Shadow Light: Illuminations at the Edge of Darkness.*

Whatever combinations of practices you try, I suggest you continue the ones that evoke joy, insight, love, and intimacy. Practice them enough and they become traits, which often include expanding perceptual capacities that can guide us to cool new states.

THE INTEGRAL STEALTH AGENDA OF *Shadow Light* AND THE *Shadow Light Workbook*

I have a stealth agenda in both *Shadow Light* and *The Shadow Light Workbook.* I am an Integrally informed therapist who has been lit up and transformed by Ken Wilber's work on the Integral meta-theory since I first encountered it. I've often had trouble teaching the system outright—it's difficult to grasp at first and people sometimes turn away before they truly get it.

For that reason, I speak *from* Integral understanding and constructs constantly throughout *Shadow Light* and *The Shadow Light Workbook*, and *about* Integral by name rarely. My hope is that you the reader will be entertained and intrigued enough to check out any of Ken Wilber's work (I especially recommend *Integral Psychology, Integral Spirituality,* and the *Kosmic Consciousness* audio series) for a deeper dive into the Integral meta-theory. If you stick with it, you'll be glad you did!

If you are a psychotherapist (or an interested non-therapist), I have included an appendix that goes deeper into this and related clinical issues at the end of this workbook.

1

SHADOW EVERYWHERE

S hadow, the unknown, is an incredible resource! We can develop and harness our Shadow to serve us and the world.

You can endlessly keep discovering your strengths and owning them, while noticing your mistakes and weaknesses and transforming them. In the process you grow your Shadow, developing a nonconscious self who increasingly dialysizes destructive thoughts and impulses into constructive ones before they even reach conscious awareness.

FRACTAL BOUNDARIES

In nature, boundaries that both separate and connect—like sand and sea, air and water, cell membranes, or between known and unknown—are called fractal boundaries. Fractals are self-replicating or self-similar patterns that occur at such boundaries, endlessly repeating at different time and/or size scales, generating endless new configurations—*new configurations biased toward creating more complex, stable, and coherent forms.*

Focus on what you're feeling in your body right now and you're going to the fractal interface between your conscious awareness and sensations/emotions/thoughts ("sensations/emotions/thoughts" because no sensation when it rises to awareness is divorced from an emotional experience and a story supporting the experience).

EXERCISE 1A

ATTUNEMENT HARMONIZES FRACTAL INTERFACES

- In the spaces provided in this workbook, I encourage you to record this and future experiences during exercises. You can also get a separate journal if you'd prefer not to write in the workbook itself. Writing about experiences and sharing them amplifies their effects.

- Sit or stand comfortably and breathe in deeply (feel your belly expand). Breathe out slowly, paying attention to every nuance of breath. Do this five to ten times until you create a rhythm of slow breathing in and out.

- Direct your attention to what you are feeling in your body right now, what you are thinking as you read this, imagining as you consider this, wanting as you become self-aware of desires, or judging as you notice judgments about others and yourself.

- Now observe all this—breath, sensations, emotions, thoughts, judgments, and impulses—with loving acceptance and caring intent.

- Think of someone you are critical of, irritated by, or you find threatening. Observe yourself being critical or irritated with acceptance and caring intent.

- Think of some aspect of yourself that you're critical of—your weight, temper, shameful secret, or guilty pleasure. Observe yourself being critical or ashamed with acceptance and caring intent.

- You probably notice a calming effect of observing these upsetting judgments with acceptance and caring intent. This is your conscious self holding your light and dark simultaneously in accepting awareness—creating a state of attunement.

- The instant these sensations, feelings, thoughts, judgments, and desires arise into conscious awareness you are at fractal boundaries between Shadow and light—boundaries you can focus on, ignore, embrace, reject, or guide with acceptance and caring intent toward harmony with your sense of self and all the stories you have about the world. Write in your journal about what you discover doing this attunement.

- Notice how such compassionate attention soothes and relaxes you. This is you sending caring attention to fractal interfaces and creating feedback loops into your non-conscious, adding compassion to experience as you reevaluate it.

- Compassionate attention shapes your non-conscious—literally accelerating the maturation of your Shadow self. One major reflector of maturation is increasing compassionate understanding of yourself, others, and the world.

- Do this five minutes a day and you will become wiser, your brain will grow (especially your right frontal lobe), and you will feel more joy and less anxiety. You will be directing yourself to the fractal interfaces of unknown arising into the known, coloring it with acceptance and caring intent, and positively influencing both your current thoughts and behavior and your future Shadow offerings.

- Write at least a few sentences describing your experiences each time you attune, and, after a week of entries, share what you've written with someone you trust. Write about your conversation afterward in your workbook. We can use flavors of emotional experience to guide us to perceive fractal boundaries between known and unknown, and adjust them to more compassion and deeper consciousness—greater complexity.

_____

_____

_____

_____

_____

_____

_____

_____

_____

_____

_____

_____

_____

_____

_____

_____

_____

_____

_____

This enables us to begin with an emotional/sensory/ideational experience—the flavor—and know that as we inquire into it with compassionate understanding we'll encounter integrative and creative opportunities in the Shadow material that emerges.

EXERCISE 1B
EXPAND YOUR EMOTIONAL PALLET

- Notice and cultivate the "flavors" of any emotion you experience during the day. What do you feel in your body as you have this emotion? What is your name for this feeling—positive or negative, pleasurable or painful? Examples are compassion, fear, shame, anger, grief, avarice, desire, disgust, interest, joy, understanding, anxiety, depression, collaborative intimacy, subtle interpersonal conflict, or confusion. A least several times a day, write down what you're feeling and where in your body you experience it. Include whether you experienced it with acceptance and caring intent, or if you resisted, denied, or attacked yourself or someone else—even if the attack was just in your own mind.

- At the end of the day, read what you've written and write how the emotion fit into whatever was happening with you individually and/or with someone else at the time. In retrospect, was the emotion proportionate? Was it disproportionate? Either way, write about it.

- After a week, look over what you've written and consider whether or not you are more aware in any way of emotion and sensation. Is there any difference in how accepting you are of emotion and sensation after practicing this? Write about this in your journal.

- Share what you've written with someone you trust and then write about your conversation.

2

WE EXIST IN A
RELATIONAL
UNIVERSE

WHERE'S MY SHADOW AND WHAT DO I DO ABOUT IT?

Let's return briefly to the fractal interfaces we discussed in Chapter One. In complex systems there are differentiated parts, which are linked. The places they are linked are fractal boundaries. Fractal boundaries both separate and connect. At these boundaries are self-repeating patterns that keep appearing with creative variations at different time and size scales. The creative variations are biased toward greater complexity—enduring new patterns, which are more energy efficient and stable (less chaotic) while still being fluid and dynamic (less rigid). If we keep examining these fractal interfaces in ourselves, we ultimately reach fields interacting with fields—*most of them guided to some extent by consciousness.*

As I mentioned earlier, a human superpower we all share is our capacity for focused intent and action, in service of principle, and driven by resolve. This superpower applied optimally to personal health and growth is ultimately using consciousness to harmonize the fractal boundaries of fields that determine our interior and interpersonal lives.

What are examples of this? You have moment-to-moment fractal boundaries between:

- Your conscious self and your multitude of inner selves in the past, present, and future.
- You and other people.
- You and nature.
- Your body and your awareness of your body.
- You and your drives and instincts.
- You and your fantasies/values/assumptions and worldviews.

Write about how you experience one of these (or some other) fractal boundaries that are important in your life.

_____

_____

_____

_____

_____

_____

_____

_____

_____

EXERCISE 2A
FRACTAL INTERFACES IN YOURSELF

- Focus on your bodily sensation for a moment. Start from your toes, and notice any sensations from your feet to the top of your head. Just sit with bodily sensation for a few seconds. This is a fractal interface between your conscious awareness and your bodily sensation.

- Now, think how grateful you are to be alive, to have a body that works in so many millions of ways—blood vessels, heart, digestive system, kidneys, brain, bones, immune system, etc. Concentrate on this until you can feel a sense of gratitude in your chest area for your amazing body—over 500 trillion cells, organized into you. Let the sense of gratitude expand as you breathe slowly in and out from your abdomen. Continue this for at least sixty seconds.

- As you do this, what changes about your awareness of your bodily sensation? You probably feel differently than when you started the exercise. What is that difference? I personally feel more of a sense of compassionate acceptance for my precious human body, and gratitude that it works as well as it does. Write about your experience in as much detail as possible.

- Repeat the exercise on at least three different days, and then share what you've written with someone you trust, writing about the conversation afterward.

- If you practice this exercise daily whenever you are aware of a bodily sensation, your conscious (and non-conscious) sense of physical coherence will expand. If you continue long enough, your Shadow will grow to the point it will naturally generate bodily awareness and gratitude much of the time.

- You have just used your human superpower of focused intent and action (concentration on sensation and gratitude), in service of principle (compassionate acceptance and gratitude are optimal), and driven by resolve (it required some willpower to do this exercise).

- You extended attention to the fractal interface between conscious awareness and bodily sensation, and biased it toward compassionate acceptance and gratitude. You just trained your Shadow to be a bit wiser and more highly integrated.

EXERCISE 2B
FRACTAL INTERFACES WITH OTHERS

- Remember an enjoyable interaction you've had with someone in the last day or two. As you look back on it, pay attention to how many ways you were connected, and where the separation was between you and this other—the interface between you and them. For instance there is a felt sense of emotional connection during an enjoyable interaction. Where is the boundary between you and the other person—where you stop and they begin? Is it equidistant between you two, simply the space between your two bodies, or some other sense of boundary? Is there any sensation or emotion involved? Write about this.

- Remember an uncomfortable interaction you've had with someone in the last day or two. Remember back to it and pay attention to how many ways you were connected, and where the separation was between you and this other. Often there is a felt sense of emotional connection during uncomfortable interactions that we instinctively avoid or deny. For instance, I've heard, "No! I'm not angry!" in countless couples' sessions. Where is the boundary between you and the other person—where you stop and they begin? Is it equidistant between you two, simply the space between your two bodies, or some other sense of boundary? Is there any sensation or emotion involved? Write about this.

- After you've done the proceeding two activities, spend a day noticing your connections with other people—the felt sense, the places where you stop and they begin. Write about this with an emphasis on what changes when you focus on the connections between you.

- Share this with someone you trust and write about your conversation.

_____

_____

_____

EXERCISE 2C
INTERSUBJECTIVITY

- The feeling between two or more people is called intersubjectivity by psychologists, and constitutes fractal boundaries that automatically form when people relate. When we send our attention to them we change them. If we send compassionate attention, we tend to change them for the better. If we send frightened, hostile, or distressed attention, we tend to change them for the worse.
- Write about at least one episode of you changing a connection for the better with love or compassion, and one where you changed it for the worse with fear, anger, shame, guilt, disgust, or any other painful affect.
- Share what you've written with someone you trust and write about the conversation.

_____

_____

_____

_____

_____

_____

_____

_____

3
THE NEUROBIOLOGY OF SHADOW—CONCEPTION TO DEATH

Can you remember your first kiss? If you glance around right now, is there anything in your immediate environment that catches your attention? Can you imagine the next time you are going to walk outside into the sunlight? Think about these three things at once—first kiss, something you notice as you glance around, and the next time you'll walk in the sunlight. As you do this, you are consciously living simultaneously in the past, present, and future—you are practicing another human superpower! No other being in the known universe can do this. Only we humans can consciously be aware of ourselves across time.

When humans developed the abilities to live simultaneously in the past, present, and future, they also could *worry about* the past, present, and future, and to empathically resonate with others' worrying. This wrecked our natural mammalian nature of not stressing if there's no current problem. The relaxed satisfaction of a grizzly bear satiated in a blueberry field, the mindless contentment of a field mouse snug in her burrow, or the timeless oneness with nature the deer feels standing motionless in the deep forest were all compromised by human memories of past pain and anticipation of future pain.

Everyone has become lost in superheated recollections of past threats and offenses. *Everyone* occasionally focuses on and amplifies current threats and offenses. Worst of all, everyone has lost sleep and been utterly distracted anticipating future threats and offenses. Such obsessions block instinctual unity with nature unless we become deep enough to remain present and open in the current moment, *while maintaining contact with the past and future.*

Integrated states where the present moment is enhanced by past/future memory and fantasy are also human birthrights (making it completely worthwhile to give up naive mammalian innocence). Such integrated states usually require life-long self-development. Key to this process is living so fully in the present moment that we harmonize with the worried ancestral voices calling urgently about past, present, and future threats—especially future threats since emotions are always *priming us to deal with what's next.*

Worrying about something in the future is called, "anticipatory anxiety." Anticipatory anxiety diminishes consciousness—it is the great enemy of development, the fly in the evolutionary ointment, the Everest to climb on the journey to enlightenment. The remedy for anticipatory anxiety is *presence.*

THE MONK AND THE TIGER

One of my favorite Buddhist stories involves a Zen Monk walking through a verdant forest and suddenly encountering a tiger, bent down low to the ground, ready to spring. Frightened for his life, the Monk takes off with the tiger in pursuit. Seeing a precipice ahead, the Monk—preferring a fall to being mauled—leaps out into the chasm. In the nick of time, he grabs a vine, leaving him clinging to the side of the mountain. As he hangs against the jungle cliff, two mice come out of a hole and begin nibbling at the vine he hanging from. Raising his eyes, he sees the tiger on the cliff's edge growling horrifically. Catching a delicate fragrance from a tiny fissure in the rock face, he sees a lone strawberry plant with a beautiful strawberry on it growing in a little pocket of soil. He reaches out and plucks the strawberry, puts it in his mouth, and slowly eats it, delighted and absorbed in sweet taste, texture, and unity with nature.

PRESENCE

I love this monk. I want to embrace each moment just like he does hanging on that cliff. Contemplative practice, receiving influence from those who love us, reaching for the highest good—they all guide us to *presence*. I encourage daily practices that foster all forms of presence. Absorption in the present moment, surrender to radiant love, and unity with pure consciousness are three of my favorites.

EXERCISE 3A
TRY PRESENCE RIGHT NOW

- Take a deep breath and relax your body.
- Feel your feet, legs, pelvis, torso, belly, chest, throat, neck, arms, hands, face, and head with acceptance.
- Be aware of all your senses—sounds, clothes on your skin, wind in your hair, sun on your back, tightness or looseness in your body . . . experience all—with acceptance and compassion.
- Relax into this state of global awareness of right now with calm acceptance and maintain it for two minutes. As you finish, move into your day with the intent to continually adjust toward global awareness with calm acceptance. Write about your experiences and, after a few entries, share them with someone you trust. Then write about your conversation.

Presence, compassion, and depth of consciousness lead us to observe what's right and beautiful. They guide us in feeling emotions and sensations, compassionately observing the associated stories and impulses, and then acting on what feels best to make good things happen. When we lose our way in defensive states or bad habits, depth of consciousness can bring us back to full presence, where all feelings are priceless guides.

This integrates our brains and grows our Shadow!

_____

_____

_____

_____

_____

4
NEUROBIOLOGY INFORMS
SHADOW WORK

Psychological defenses are necessary to help us thrive. We need instincts to warn and guide us when our nervous systems read danger, and our nervous systems are incredibly sensitive. If I show you an angry face for 40 milliseconds (less than a tenth of a second), you'll have no conscious awareness that anything has happened, while your nervous system registers fear—your Shadow warning and guiding you. Your adaptive unconscious has determined threat and is priming you with fear to fight or flee if the threat intensifies—all out of conscious awareness, all in Shadow.

Of course, to a large extent, our psychological defenses, established as reflexes from conception onward, often cause suffering due to their primitive origins and habitual natures, rising reflexively as they do from destructive Shadow at the least hint of threat.

Defensive states inevitably involve amplified or numbed emotions, distorted perspectives, destructive impulses, and diminished capacities for empathy and self-reflection—practically never optimal reactions to most situations.

Working with defenses is always at the edge of awareness—always Shadow work. Much Shadow work directs awareness to defensive barriers—fractal boundaries—where we resist perception of critical judgments, forbidden passions, and self-destructive defensive states. With the help of guides like our own interior principles and wise others, we can penetrate those barriers, find the material and refine our values to become increasingly relativistic and mature. As we do that we become more coherent neurobiologically.

IDENTIFYING AND REGULATING DEFENSIVE STATES

Remember the last time you were personally in conflict with someone you were relatively close to (a spouse, child, parent, good friend, coworker, or manager are all possibilities). You are face to face, distressed, observing the other feeling bad and feeling bad yourself. Usually there is some sense of anger or threat involved, but not always. Sometimes there is despair, helplessness, blankness, frustration, guilt, shame, or excitement (some arguments or rants can feel exhilarating or cathartic). I remember ranting at a friend whom I thought had made a big mistake advising my wife Becky many years ago. I was super mad, thought my friend was completely wrong, didn't care that my hostile tone was hurting her, and was unaware of how over-the-top nasty I was being. In retrospect, I imagine she was feeling anger and fear, had beliefs about me being unreasonable and abusive, and couldn't wait to get away from our conversation.

_____

_____

_____

_____

_____

_____

EXERCISE 4A
OBSERVING THE OTHER'S DEFENSIVE STATE

- Write about the emotions you observe in this other person during this remembered conflict. Emotions are not thoughts; they are based in sensations and can usually be expressed in one word like irritation, anxiety, rage, fear, guilt, or disgust, always connected to a physical experience. For instance, anger often involves heat or tension in the heart area. Fear often involves a distressed—even nauseous—feeling in the solar plexus and gut.

- Write about the emotions/sensations you observe (or imagine) this person feeling in detail. In your opinion were these emotions amplified or numbed in some fashion—disproportionate to what the actual event was? Write about this.

- What are the beliefs this other person seems to be having about you, the conflict, and themselves? These beliefs include their perspectives about what you're conflicted about, but also what they seem to be believing about you as you—your worth or personal qualities. Do these beliefs seem distorted in any way? Write about all this.

- How able is this other person to compassionately observe themselves or empathically resonate with you? Do they seem to know exactly what emotions, thoughts, and messages they're putting out, or do they seem off base? Do you feel compassionately empathized with, or misunderstood? Write about all this.

- What impulses does this person seem to be following in this conflict? Are they impulses to cooperate and empathically resonate, or impulses to attack, defend, or reject? Write about these.

_____

_____

_____

EXERCISE 4B
OBSERVING YOUR DEFENSIVE STATE

- Write about the emotions you observe in yourself during this conflictual encounter. Emotions are not thoughts; they are based in sensations and can usually be expressed in one word like irritation, anxiety, rage, fear, guilt, or disgust, always connected to a physical experience. For instance, anger often involves heat or tension in your heart area. Fear often involves a distressed—even nauseous—feeling in your solar plexus and gut. Write about the emotions/sensations in detail. In your opinion are they amplified or numbed in some fashion—disproportionate to what the actual even is? Write about this in as much detail as possible.

- What are the beliefs you have in this conflict? These include your perspectives about what you're conflicted about, but also what you are believing about you and this other person. In retrospect, do these beliefs seem distorted in any way? Write about all this.

- During this encounter, how able were you to compassionately observe yourself or empathically resonate with the other person's perspectives and distress? Do you believe you knew exactly what emotions, thoughts, and messages you were feeling and putting out, or, in retrospect, do you seem off base in your sense of self and other? Did the other person feel compassionately empathized with, or misunderstood? Write about all this.

- What impulses did you have in this conflict? Were they impulses to cooperate and empathically resonate, impulses to attack, defend, or reject, or combinations of impulses? Write about these.

_____

_____

_____

_____

You've just described the defensive states you and this other person activated during your conflict. *Just observing* these dimensions *as they happen* liberates you to some extent from blindly trusting amplified or numbed emotions, completely believing distorted perspectives, indulging destructive impulses, or allowing yourself to compromise your abilities for empathy and self-reflection.

When you self-observe, you are self-regulating to some extent. This is especially true for defensive states because none of us wants to do damage to intimates or ourselves when we're upset, and all of us feel better when we can shift destructive Shadow influences to constructive Shadow programming.

In my own example I cited earlier about the friend I ranted at when I believed she gave Becky bad advice, I felt guilty after my rant and tried to contact my friend to repair. She felt too injured from our talk to even consider discussing it further with me. A five-minute rant ended a valuable friendship, and taught me a lesson in challenging defensive states that has stayed with me ever since—they are dangerous and require mature attention or we risk practicing bad habits, causing unnecessary harm, and even losing valuable relationships.

TURNING PROCRASTINATION INTO STRENGTH

Knowing we don't want to reinforce turning away from responsibility, that it's best to face resistance and take assertive action, that doing so strengthens non-conscious neurological constructive Shadow programming, we can use our human superpowers of focused intent and action in service of principle, and driven by resolve to use each impulse to procrastinate as a cue for powerful, responsible action. This turns the liability of procrastination into the strength of mature action.

_____

_____

_____

PROCRASTINATION INTO STRENGTH

Pay attention to when you procrastinate throughout the day and write what you discover in your workbook.

- After two days of this, pick one activity you commonly procrastinate on—like doing the dishes, answering email, taking out the recycling, or kissing your husband—and do it **every time you are aware you're procrastinating.** Use your impulse to procrastinate as a signal to actually engage in the activity you're resisting.

- After a week of using the impulse to procrastinate to actually get things accomplished, write how you feel differently about yourself, the tasks, and procrastination in general.

- Share what you've written with someone you trust. Write about your conversation.

_____

_____

_____

_____

_____

_____

_____

5

ARCHETYPAL SHADOW: THE HERO'S DESCENT INTO THE WELL OF THE WORLD

Who's your favorite superhero? Frodo? Superman? Albert Einstein? Carl Jung? Plato? Jesus? Buddha? Mother Teresa? Yoda? Bill Gates? Barak Obama? The hero from your favorite book?

Who's your worst villain? Hitler? The Joker? Dracula? Your-most-hated-politician? The mean girls from junior high? Al Johnson who bullied you in high school?

All these attractive and repulsive archetypal figures evoke strong reactions in you, and thus reveal Shadow material about your type of person. Who we are is often best revealed by what attracts and repulses us.

_____

_____

_____

_____

EXERCISE 5A
SUPERHEROES AS MIRRORS

- Write down five superheroes—real or fictional characters—you particularly are drawn to.
- Now write two or three qualities that you admire in each of them. Take all these qualities and put them in a column on the left side of the page.
- Opposite them, on the right side, write where you have embodied—or wished you had embodied—each quality at some time. Courage, compassion, self-sacrifice, intuitive genius, physical strength, deep understanding, etc.
- Now, write down five villains—real or fictional characters—you personally can't stand.
- Next to each write two or three qualities that most characterize each of them.
- Take all these qualities and put them in a column on the left side of another page, and on the right side write where you have embodied each quality at some time. Cowardice, selfishness, violence, bullying, victimizing, self-indulgence, cluelessness, bigotry, idiotic bad judgment, etc.
- These two sheets together are a representation of many of your constructive and destructive Shadow forces. You have a scaffolding of qualities that comprise your unique type of person.
- Share this with someone you trust, and record what you learned and experienced in the conversation.

_____

_____

_____

_____

A HERO NEEDS A MISSION

You'll notice that all your heroes and villains have missions most of the time. The villains' missions are usually self-aggrandizement or destruction, and the heroes' missions are usually service to others or self-transcendence (as in seekers wanting deeper connections with Spirit, or athletes completely dedicated to being the best they can be). You are the hero in your epic journey—what is *your* mission?

EXERCISE 5B
WHAT IS YOUR CURRENT MISSION?

- How do you want to further embody your positives and transform your negatives? What would you like to accomplish doing this besides becoming a more integrated, powerful, and whole person? In other words, do you have a mission? Some service you want to provide to your family, community, country, or the world? Some artifact or art you want to create? Some goal you urgently wish to accomplish? Write these down.

- After you do all this, look at this sheet and the two others from the previous exercise as a whole, a framework of your strengths, weaknesses, yearnings, shames, and passions. Is there a theme? Is there a mission? Is there purpose? If you find any of these, you have a beginning road map for your Hero's journey, perhaps even a call!

_____

_____

_____

_____

_____

_____

_____

WE ARE ALL BATMAN AND WONDER WOMAN. NOW WHAT?

Myths arise endlessly from each of us and all of us. Archetypal forms emerge from human collectives, informing all of us whether we know it or not.

Archetypes influence us in multiple ways. Primary influences are simply which archetypes compel us. This is completely personal. When my wife Becky was asked at ten-years-old what she wanted to be she said, "A Mommy." The Mother archetype lit her up (in Greek mythology this is Hestia, the Goddess of the Hearth). When I asked her in her twenties what she wanted, she responded from her Seeker self, "I want to expand my consciousness," the path of Woman of Wisdom lit her up (Hera in the Greek, Shakti in the Hindu, Changing Woman in the Navajo).

Secondary effects arise from negotiating archetypal demands and influences with culture. Culture is quite friendly to some archetypes, and incredibly hostile to others.

A woman who resonates powerfully with the Sex Goddess will have inner conflicts and bewildering shame if raised in a fundamentalist, anti-sexuality family or community. Her yummy Sex Goddess self feels sinful, shame surges.

Similarly, Women of Wisdom have had to mask or turn away from their power in families and cultures that suppress women. The last eight thousand years of agrarian societies have been hard on acknowledging and supporting women in general and Women of Wisdom in particular (who've had to handle a lot of clueless and dangerous men just to survive).

My maternal grandfather was a Warrior raised in a Quaker culture. When he volunteered to fight in WWI he was the first in three generations to go to war, probably not popular with some of his family and congregation.

If our cultural surround celebrates a central archetype, it's great!

The Athena athlete warrior princess archetype is often encouraged and admired by parents who delight in her striving and courage. Serena Williams, for instance, was supported this way first by her family and then by the world.

The Maiden and Divine Lover tend to be supported by families who value beauty and sensuality. They're encouraged to blossom and thrive toward warm community and happy families.

Honorable Husband and Wise Father archetypes are supported by most families and communities.

The star quarterback who resolves to help his teammates be better and to keep improving himself is celebrated by his school and community.

Our personal and cultural archetypes constantly influence us both consciously and non-consciously. Our Shadow selves *inform us* from the values and passions of our personal constellations of archetypal figures and stories.

What archetypes turn you on or repel you? Both reveal your basic nature and your current address on the epic journey of your life. We discover ourselves by what attracts or repels us in:

- Books, plays, or movies.
- Games, sports, competitions.
- Activities we enjoy or are repelled by including recreational and professional ones.
- Friends—whom we choose, who chooses us, and how we relate.
- Family members, lovers, in-laws and other tribal members.
- Fetishes, obsessions, night-dreams (especially repetitive dreams), and daydreams.
- Attributions, blessings, condemnations, and inspirations toward and from others.
- Characters/themes/relationships/missions that move us in some fashion.

All these and more reflect our archetypal Shadow influences.

_____

_____

_____

_____

EXERCISE 5C
FIND YOUR PERSONAL MYTHOS THROUGH
FEELINGS, DREAMS, AND DIALOGUE

- Write about what draws you in (attracts and enlivens you) and pushes you away (repulses or disgusts you).
- In addition, write your dreams each morning, complete with characters, themes, and emotions.
- Every month review what you've written and share your thoughts and insights with someone you trust. Write about these conversations.
- Over time your mythic constellation—your person mythos—will become clearer and clearer. As it does, write about your discoveries, share them with someone you trust, and write about your conversations.

_____

_____

_____

_____

_____

_____

_____

_____

_____

_____

_____

_____

_____

_____

_____

_____

_____

_____

_____

_____

_____

_____

_____

_____

_____

As we discover ourselves, our archetypes emerge from shadow into the light, where we can consciously shape them as we wish. Authentic growth is always in keeping with our deeper purpose, life missions, and intimate relationships—constantly revealed to us in constructive Shadow. Disease is disconnection, self-betrayal, turning away from healthy intimacy and self-knowledge—revealed to us in destructive Shadow.

The hero and heroine's journey reflects these processes for men and women, for masculine and feminine.

6
WARRIOR AND MAN OF WISDOM

The Warrior and Man of Wisdom find themselves in relationships with others. Warrior/Man of Wisdom values are enacted in relationship with others. Thus growth as Warrior and Man of Wisdom is often intertwined with our increasing capacities to relate courageously and compassionately in even the most difficult circumstances. How can we support such growth?

HOW TO HELP YOUR WARRIOR AND
MAN OF WISDOM GROW

I suggest you take this workbook to a private place that feels beautiful and comfortable to you.

- Remember a time you were extremely angry and acted badly by your standards, and write it down in detail.
- Remember a time you were extremely angry and acted well by your standards, and write it down in detail.
- Remember a time you were extremely fearful or anxious and acted badly by your standards, and write it down in detail.
- Remember a time you were extremely fearful or anxious and acted well by your standards, and write it down in detail.
- Imagine yourself facing the younger you that acted well and say something to him (like "I admire your wisdom and courage in the clutch"). Observe his imagined expression. How is he responding in words or actions? Write down everything you experience.
- Imagine yourself facing the younger you that acted badly through fear or anger. What are you most deeply moved to say to him right now? It might be something like, "I'm ashamed of what you did," or "I'm frightened of you." Say it to him in your imagination, and observe how his imagined expression changes or how he responds in words or actions. Write down what you experience.
- Continue these dialogues daily for a week, writing down what happens and what you learn.
- Share everything with someone you trust and write what comes of the conversation.

_____

_____

Exercise 6B
CULTIVATE THE WISE WITNESS

- The "you" who just talked to your younger self is probably deeper, wiser, and more courageous than your younger self. Resolve to be this deeper self more minutes of every day—not thinking about being this wiser self, but actually embodying and being your wiser self, looking through his eyes and speaking with his voice.

- As you move through your life, keep noticing when you act well or badly by your standards and give yourself the same attention you gave yourself in the previous exercise. Write about this and share it with someone you trust, and as usual, write about your conversations.

- These practices will amplify your Warrior nature and accelerate your development into Man of Wisdom.

WHAT ARE YOUR SACRED TEXTS?

What books speak deep truths to you. What are your principles that resonate with their teaching and are guided by their wisdom?

EXERCISE 6C
EXPLORE YOUR SACRED TEXT FOR YOUR PRINCIPLES

- Sacred texts are any writing that speaks to our hearts with values we want to live by, either directly like, "Though shall not kill!" or metaphorically like the theme of our favorite story. Write principles from your sacred text (or texts) in a list and put down next to each one how committed you are to living that principle using a rating scale of 1 (barely committed) to 10 (fully committed).
- Read what you've written daily.
- In two weeks rate how you feel about each again, assigning new 1 to 10 scores. Are you more or less committed? Share this with someone you trust and write about the conversation.

_____

_____

_____

_____

_____

_____

_____

_____

TWO RULES FOR GUYS—DON'T BE A DICK, DON'T BE A PUSSY

I've done three TEDx talks, and the last one, *Two Rules for Guys*, was essentially a shorthand approach to being the Warrior (check it out at https://www. youtube.com/watch?v=T5YZ9CttznE). Rule number one is, "Don't be a dick!" If you are bullying other people you might be using your power, but probably not in service of your principles (unless you have a principle that it's a great thing to bully other people). Bullies actually have a lot of self-esteem, but they don't have a lot of self-awareness, their relationships suck, and they tend to be unhappy. That's the first rule for guys—*Don't be a dick!*

Rule number two is, *"Don't be a pussy!"* You're a pussy if you allow somebody to dominate you inappropriately. If you say, "Yes," when you want to say, "No," you are collapsing. If you don't stand up for your principles—don't take your stand with, "This is what's right," in the face of something you believe is wrong—you surrender to external coercion and become a pussy. Often in such cases, the rational is, "My boss made me do it," "My wife insisted," "I couldn't help it," etc.

We've seen such collapses a lot in the last twenty or thirty years in the political arena. People who come out of an administration often write a book and say, "Well, the decisions I made (going to war, lying, hurting poor people, surrendering to special interests) went against my principles, but I did it because I was ordered to."

"I was just following orders" is what the world was contemptuous of in the Nuremberg trials of Nazi war criminals. But it's interesting how often that gets pulled out by somebody working for some boss or institution that violates personal principles. So if you have a principle, don't violate it. If you do violate it, you suffer—*don't be a pussy!*

LET YOUR WARRIOR AND MAN OF WISDOM HELP WITH YOUR DICK AND PUSSY SELVES

- Remember a time you felt deeply ashamed in relationship with another. Be your Warrior self-observing your ashamed self and give yourself feedback on that episode.
- Now be your Man of Wisdom self-observing your shamed self and give yourself feedback.
- Check in daily with your Warrior self and Man of Wisdom self. Each day have dialogues between you and your Warrior and Man of Wisdom and write about your experiences. As you become familiar with being your Warrior and Man of Wisdom, try inhabiting those selves at work, at home, and with friends.
- After two weeks, share everything with someone you trust, and write about the conversation.

_____

_____

_____

_____

_____

_____

_____

7

MANY PATHS TO
WOMAN OF WISDOM

Woman of Wisdom is much like Man of Wisdom, and this is not surprising. Healthy development with all people converges toward common principles and capacities. For instance, little girls' moral frameworks lean toward *care* for others, while little boys' moral frameworks lead toward *rights* for others. As they mature morally, the "others" group for both males and females expands beyond themselves to include family, tribe, nation, humanity as a whole, and life itself—this is a predictable moral progression. The upper levels of both men's and women's moral development involves felt concern *for both rights and care for all.*

So, like the Man of Wisdom, the Woman of Wisdom:

- **Is grateful for what is.**
- **Discerns love and truth from BS,** "Perceives those things which cannot be seen," as Miyamoto Musashi said about the Warrior.
- **Harmonizes relationships** within herself (including her Shadow and inner masculine) and her relationships with her masculine partner, others, her purpose, and the world.
- **Is confident in her principles and the Way.**
- **Is in tune with the deeper rhythms** of when to surrender and when to take a stand. She respects the masculine but doesn't fear the masculine, and so can access it in herself and enjoy it in men.

- **Woman of Wisdom perspectives broaden as she develops**, making her progressively more relativistic where intuitive knowledge of the highest good can instantaneously transform her opinions and actions.
- **The Woman of Wisdom has compassionate understanding** with intuitive knowledge of everything. She's moved to channel spiritually correct truths and directions into the world.
- A **Woman of Wisdom** lives in love—the universe is saturated with love which informs everything.
- **As she matures toward Woman of Wisdom**, actions and beliefs that don't consider the highest good for everyone feel partial and unsatisfying. Actions and beliefs that do seek the highest good become more obvious and essential.

Even though the seeds of Woman of Wisdom exist in all women, we grow through stages and archetypes toward this integrated self. No one starts out at Woman of Wisdom the same way infants don't start out as fully-grown adults. As we wake up to ourselves as children, adolescents, and grownups, certain paths shine with more luminance. Following these paths to best serve love leads to Woman of Wisdom.

Let's explore some of the most common archetypal forms that light up and inform women.

The Handless Maiden discovers herself not anchored in her power and autonomous authority, seemingly helpless in the face of the world's demands, judgments, and coercions. In spite of her felt helplessness, she can courageously embrace the Heroine's Journey when called by yearning, disaster, circumstance, or relationship. By looking inward, receiving guidance and help, and surrendering to her deepest soul and wise guides, she can eventually discover herself as the Woman of Wisdom, but the forces of powerlessness and helplessness will always periodically arise as destructive Shadow that demands attention and integration.

The Ingénue ("Puella" is the Jungian name) is the darling of the ball, the eternal radiant young goddess of purity and love. She can offer her innocence to the world—opening to love and closing to violence—allowing herself to gradually be transformed into Woman of Wisdom. Her development is learning to discern innocence from naiveté, spontaneity from narcissistic self-absorption, and devotional love from unhealthy dependence. Awakening to these forces arising out of Shadow guides her toward Woman of Wisdom.

The Sex Goddess can mobilize her power, channel sensual/erotic pleasure into the world—often becoming the Divine Lover to her chosen partner—progressing from serving her own hungers and cultural demands to leading the tribe in passionate embodiment—the Woman of Wisdom.

The Divine Mother dedicates herself to children thriving—seeing Spirit in each moment of every child's life. She supports, guides, and adjusts to children's shifting needs, even as she supports, guides, and adjusts to her partner, her family, and her own growth. Her children thrive, individuate, and co-construct unique lives with her and others. As she adjusts and responds with love to the ever shifting demands, she transforms into Woman of Wisdom.

The Divine Wife surrenders to love with a trustable man. She shows him her suffering at his collapses and her delight at his integrity and presence. She empowers herself and is committed to empowering him. She commits to supporting her own and her man's fulfillment emotionally, sexually, and spiritually. She is often the gatekeeper to their social networks, organizing and discerning what serves everyone best. In partnership with her beloved she moves into Woman of Wisdom.

The Healer harnesses her native desires to care with nature's hunger for balance and harmony. She finds her healing modes and allows them to grow in her as she serves the world. As she practices her healing gifts, her confidence expands, her connections with the other world stabilize, and she becomes the Woman of Wisdom.

Huntress/athlete (Athena in Greek Mythology) harnesses physical strength and courage with penetrating insight. She is drawn to striving and conflict in service of competition (think Olympic athletes or Mixed Martial Arts champion Rhonda Rousey), or protection (think Zena, Warrior Princess). The Goddess Athena was generally portrayed as a virgin—I assume partly because the complexity of combining Athena Warrior Feminine with Aphrodite (Goddess of love—devotional erotic surrender to the beloved) was too much of a reach for ancient Greeks. Current post-modern cultures include dialectics like Warrior domination and feminine devotional surrender. The kick-ass woman CEO can come home and be ravished by her strong and trustable masculine partner.

The Seeker knows intuitively that everything is Spirit, and dedicates herself to surrendering to Spirit, developing insight and power to share her spiritual light, and affiliating with like-minded others to form spiritual communities. As she progresses on her Way, she discovers herself as Woman of Wisdom.

The Artist sees beauty everywhere and is moved to generate beauty as a central calling. As she transforms inspirations into artifacts of words, objects (like food, clothes, paintings, or gardens), images, movements, relationships, experiences, or sounds, she moves toward Woman of Wisdom.

These are a sampling of core feminine archetypes. Women can channel any or all of them—with each woman a unique configuration of drives, yearnings, and experiences.

More than any other time in human history, our current era privileges individual desires and paths over conformity to external standards—even though external standards are always guiding and informing us. Western progressive cultures have normalized the idea that we grow through different identifications and passions, and we are increasingly accepting of individual variations. Thinking developmentally helps us understand how expanding any level of expertise/discernment leads through progressive interpenetrating archetypes toward Woman of Wisdom. I've observed many such paths with extraordinary women I've known and worked with over the years.

EXERCISE 7A
WHAT ARE MY CURRENT ARCHETYPES?

- Write down the archetypes I've described in a column.
- After each one, give it a score from -5 (minus 5) where you just can't stand her, to +5 (plus 5) where you totally love her. Zero is you being completely indifferent, though we are rarely completely indifferent about anything.
- When you're done look at your ratings, especially the highs and lows. The archetypes you especially like and especially hate reveal Shadow attractions and repulsions that will lead you to important parts of yourself.
- Make an effort to radically accept all your reactions and be curious about what they may tell you about your current self, life, and relationships. Write down any insights and observations.
- What you most liked, your highest scores, probably represent yearnings and personal strengths, and should be loved and cultivated.
- What you most disliked probably reflect personal Shadow you have trouble accepting and loving. If you are repulsed or put off by the Divine Mother, Sex Goddess, Warrior/athlete, or any other feminine form, you probably have Shadow resistance to them. What might your resistance be? Write about it in this workbook.
- Share everything you've written with someone you trust.

_____

_____

_____

_____

_____

EXERCISE 7B
WHAT IS MY CURRENT HEROINE'S JOURNEY?

Write down your answers to these questions.

- What stages of life am I most expressing at this time? Am I in adolescence, young womanhood, the Woman Warrior, the Sex Goddess, the lover, the Bride, the Young Mother, the Brilliant Woman Creator, the Loyal Community Member, the Feminine Leader, the Divine Mother, the Healer, the Woman of Wisdom? What most draws my attention, excites my interest, or demands my obligation? I am probably some combination of these and other archetypal forms.

- How do I move through this stage of my life being true to my responsibilities and myself?

- Inclusive boundaries are activities or behaviors I insist upon including in my life (like exercise or kissing my children goodnight), and exclusive boundaries are activities or behaviors I refuse to tolerate in my life (like domestic violence or infidelity). How do I tell what inclusive and exclusive boundaries to set for my partner, my children, friends, anyone, or me?

- What are the three most important principles that guide me?

- Who are my best guides? What input from them do I welcome and embody, and what input do I resist and refuse?

- Share all that you've written with someone you trust. Write about your conversation.

_____

_____

_____

_____

_____

_____

_____

_____

_____

_____

_____

_____

_____

_____

_____

Answering these questions guides you to your current station on your Heroine's Journey.

I especially like the approach of therapist, teacher, and mystic, Ann Davin, in her program *The Heroine's Journey*. She conceptualizes the Heroine's Journey as progressing through five phases:

- **Phase 1—Everyday Woman:** Beginning as the Handless Maiden, out of touch with her agency and hungering for self-care, self-awareness, and self-possession, a woman takes responsibility for what she experiences and does, and recognizes herself as a reflection of the divine.

- **Phase 2—Rupture:** Her Journey takes her into chaos through activating events where she is challenged to surrender to her becoming. She enters the Belly of The Whale, the Well of the World, and grieves her losses and everyone's losses. Fear and doubt, when faced, transform into spiritual courage and confidence. Through these trials she dies and is reborn into her native beauty and lively energy.

- **Phase 3—Transparency:** Rigorous self-observation expands her inner Witness, and she faces the Shadow aspects of her strengths and weaknesses, triumphs and heartbreaks, cultivating radical acceptance of all her inner selves, including the Handless Maiden. Chaos intrudes; feelings of victimization and powerlessness overwhelm and need to be faced by her with the help of guides/friends/community, which leads her to . . .

- **Phase 4—Receiving:** She says "Yes!" to love, sensuality, contact, community, and the subtle realms of dreams, visions, and Spirit in all her forms. Alison Armstrong says receptivity is the sine qua non, the deal breaker or deal maker, in a woman's relationship with a man—and I think with nature and the world also. Receive love, receive guidance, receive the pleasures of life, receive your man's finest qualities, and you advance on the Heroine's Journey. John Gottman, the world's preeminent couples' researcher, found that receiving positive influence to be one of the main characteristics of the "masters" of relationships, and a major deficit of the "disasters" of relationships.

- **Phase 5—Action:** Finding deep purpose, she expresses herself through service that restores, energizes, and transforms her. She revisits old wounds, finding power in the polarities between connection and loss, love and pain, acceptance and rejection. Codependency becomes interdependency, and her Woman of Wisdom self becomes mostly available when needed.

WHERE ARE YOU ON YOUR CURRENT HEROINE'S JOURNEY?

In your workbook answer the following questions.

- What current life activity feels the most important and meaningful to me? Is it my spiritual seeking, parenting, service, self-maintenance, self-healing, lover relationship, friends, community, art? Is it some combination of these?
- What am I currently doing to support my most important and meaningful life activities?
- What are my dreams and yearnings? Make a list that includes even your wildest fantasies.
- What am I currently doing to embody my dreams and yearnings?
- What am I currently doing to sabotage my dreams and yearnings? This could be over-commitment, fatigue, fear, self-doubt, or reluctance to ask for support and help.
- How does all of the above fit into my Heroine's Journey? What is my call, my magical aids (or potential magical aids), the threshold and threshold guardians? What obstacles and opponents in the world and myself am I currently struggling with? What different aspects of me need more acceptance, empowerment, and support? Who are the teachers and guides that most light me up right now? What is the emerging Woman of Wisdom in me like—how does she feel and how do I access her?
- Share everything you've written with someone you love.

_____

_____

_____

_____

_____

_____

_____

_____

_____

_____

_____

As we discover ourselves, as our archetypes emerge from Shadow into the light, we can consciously shape them as we wish. Growth is always in keeping with our deeper purpose, life missions, and loving relationships. Disease is disconnection, self-betrayal, turning away from healthy intimacy and self-knowledge.

8
SEXUAL SHADOW

I n the sexual occasion, most of us are more purely masculine or feminine, and this is our *sexual essence.*

Erotic engagement, like dance, requires a masculine leader and a feminine follower, and almost all of us are more drawn to being one or the other in the sexual occasion.

Sometimes men have critical judgments or conditioned disapproval about their feminine aspects, or women about their masculine aspects, which drives this material into Shadow where we respond by dissociating (becoming unaware), denying (refusing to accept a part of ourselves), or projecting/attacking (seeing this in others and hating and despising *them* to protect ourselves from acknowledging forbidden parts of ourselves). Examples are how it can be confusing and distressing to a guy who values toughness to collapse into vulnerability, or for a woman who values social harmony to ragefully kick ass.

WHAT'S MY SEXUAL SHADOW?

- Who are the consenting adults you especially despise or condemn sexually? Porn stars? Prudes? Cheaters? Masturbators? Openly gay or lesbian public displays of affection? Cross-dressers? Sadomasochism enthusiasts? Even keeping to consenting adults, the list can stretch out pretty far for many of us.

- Write about these persons or groups of people in your journal, and describe their sexuality in as much detail as possible, including how you imagine their sexual practices play out and how each person feels while he or she is having sex.

- Now read what you've written and pay attention to your body and imagination as you do. Is there a thrill anywhere? Is there a little tingle of arousal? Is there disgust or shame? Write this down, and consider how it might reflect your sexual Shadow.

- If there is some practice or image you find particularly disgusting or offensive, focus on it for a bit, and imagine yourself doing this practice with enthusiasm. What do you experience? Distress, guilt, arousal, anger at me for suggesting you do this? Write what you discover.

- Try telling yourself the following phrase about this person (or these people), "They have the right to be who they are," and see how you feel. Write about that and look for insight about you.

- Read everything you've written and look for new understanding of your own sexual Shadow. Write what you find.

- Share everything you've written with someone you trust.

_____

_____

_____

_____

_____

_____

_____

_____

_____

_____

_____

_____

_____

_____

_____

_____

The sex drive is especially complicated because, due to the shame dynamics and socialization influences, we all have aspects of our sexuality (and our partner's sexuality) that we are ashamed of, resist knowledge of, or even fear.

Further, how men and women initiate sex changes from romantic infatuation into intimate bonding, because the desire-leads-to-arousal mechanisms present in both men and women in lust and romantic infatuation often shift *in women* to arousal-leads-to-desire during intimate bonding.

During intimate bonding when sexual urgency diminishes and familiarity/routines/responsibilities accelerate, men tend to keep their desire-leads-to-arousal tendencies because they are *visually erotic*—the sight of their partner's curves and smile evokes desire-leading-to-arousal interest in sex right now.

Women in intimate bonding can have the same diminished sexual urgency and burdens of familiarity/routines/responsibilities, but often shift into *arousal-leads-to-desire* in their committed relationship. In other words, women in longer-term relationships *often don't know they want to have sex until they're having sex*. Since modern women have been taught by well meaning others to, "Say 'No,' if you don't feel like it," this can lead to gradually diminished and increasingly conflicted sex in intimately bonded relationships.

Don Symons, evolutionary psychologist, demonstrated with a series of studies that in modern relationships, women are probably the determiners of sexual frequency. Lesbian and straight couples tended to have about the same number of sexual encounters per week. Gay male couples had way more partners and sexual frequency. Whatever the frequency or sexual orientation, couples who want to remain erotically mutually fulfilled usually need to collaboratively negotiate the intimate bonding sexual challenge.

If couples can't *consciously* adapt to this new configuration, they risk losing each other as lovers.

This is probably one of the explanations for John Gottman's finding that when one partner initiates sex, the other says "No," and the initiator remains loving and positive, that the couple tends to have plenty of sex. Couples where the "No," was met with neutral or negative responses reported less and less satisfying sex.

I believe that loving response to "No," is the tip of the iceberg, revealing much more about a couple than just that one dynamic. With many couples I've worked with, a positive response to a "No" to sexual initiation indicates a comfort with initiation, with "Yes," with "No," and with a bias toward saying, "Yes" to sex in general—in other words a conscious, cooperative shared sexuality.

EXERCISE 8B
BOTH-SEXUALLY-FULFILLED

- Write the ideal formula for you and your partner to both feel sexually fulfilled. Tender words, date nights, scheduled love making, once-a-week, twice-a-week, three-times-a-week frequency, sex games—put everything on the table, and write what in your opinion would keep both of you connected and happy.

- Write which stage of relating you are in. Have you just met and are lusting for your lover? Are you passionately attached and obsessed with your lover, still in romantic infatuation territory? Have you passed into intimate bonding where you feel like intimate family but might not feel as consistently hot for each other? Do you have children under five? Five to ten? Ten to twenty? Have you progressed to middle age?

- If you are currently making a both-sexually-fulfilled formula happen, write how you and your lover are managing it.

- If you are not making this ideal formula happen, what's stopping you? Cluelessness? Mindlessness? Fatigue? Disinterest? Lack of trust? Hopelessness? Conflict? Your partner's refusal to grow sexually? Your refusal to grow? Rationalizations about sex, marriage, or your partner that seem like legitimate reasons to neglect mutual fulfillment? Write what's stopping you two from creating the ideal mutually-fulfilled formula, and especially include your part in not making the ideal happen.

- Share everything you've written with your partner, and use the conversation to create more love and sexual fulfillment in your relationships. If that doesn't happen, go see a therapist for help.

- Don't wait to see a therapist. The average couple sees a therapist six years after problems start, and that's a lot of negative momentum and regrettable incidents. Believe me, as a therapist it's a lot easier to deal with, "We've been disconnected the last two months and we want to fix it," than "We haven't had sex in five years."

_____

_____

_____

_____

_____

_____

_____

WHAT YOU LIKE CAN CHANGE WITH LEVELS OF AROUSAL

Often, you gradually get turned on, then really turned on, and then somebody has an orgasm. On average 30% of women and 75% of men have orgasms during intercourse.

Sex progresses through stages and can happen fast or slow, hard or soft, or any number of other ways. In Integral we call these "state stages" because they are a progression of related states of consciousness.

You might not like deep wet kissing in the beginning of love making, but melt into it when you're moderately or majorly turned on.

You might like soft stroking rhythms at the beginning and hard pounding rhythms at the end.

Acceptance of you and your partner is accepting what gets either of you off at different stages of sex—*while only saying "Yes" to actually doing stuff that you enjoy at least somewhat* at every stage.

"Enjoy at least somewhat," means you have no problem doing the activity, and at a minimum it's mildly pleasant, even if it doesn't particularly get *you* off. For instance, you don't have to really like biting his nipples if you *kind of like* biting them because he gets super turned on when you do.

EXERCISE 8C
CREATE A LUST MAP

- Get a big sheet of paper and put "My lust map" in a three-inch circle in the center.
- Then make wavy lines out from the center circle, and at the end of each one write something that turns you on or off—yes, what turns you off is also part of your lust map. You can use different colors, draw pictures, paste images, whatever you like.
- Keep elaborating on what turns you on and off, until you have created a personal masterpiece of a lust map.

EXERCISE: 8D
SHARE YOUR LUST MAP WITH YOUR PARTNER
OR SOMEONE YOU TRUST

- That's right! Share it, describe it, and encourage him or her to make his or her own lust map to share with you.
- If this exercise turns into major problems, find a therapist and take your maps into the sessions.
- Stay present! We are taught to dissociate from sex in ourselves and others when we're the least bit stressed. Present is attuned to yourself, attuned to your partner, and focused on radical acceptance.
- Look for constructive and destructive Shadow in your lust maps and in your conversations. What is hard to accept in you or your partner? What is disappointing? What is a pleasant or sexy surprise? Write all this in your workbook and share it with your partner. Write about the conversation.

_____

_____

_____

_____

_____

_____

_____

_____

_____

_____

_____

_____

An awful lot of input around sex—like all guys like blow jobs and all women like guys to go down on them—is not necessarily true in some people's individual lust maps—often leading us to feel weird about what we like.

We like what we like, and no couple does or likes *everything* that either one of them likes—sex is always an ongoing work in progress.

What's something you like or don't like sexually that feels weird or not normal to you? For instance, you might like to say or hear sexual words during intercourse, but that feels vaguely wrong, or you don't particularly like the missionary position and feel embarrassed or wrong. (One woman I worked with was concerned because her Catholic lover always exclaimed, "Jesus Fucking Christ!" when he had an orgasm. I encouraged her to both normalize it and talk to him about her discomfort, which she did, with the result of it fading into a non-issue.) Write about your subjectively-weird-or-not-normal sexual activity in detail in your journal.

- Discus this with your partner or someone you trust and write about the conversation.
- Do you feel more or less weird or normal after the conversation, and why? Write your reactions.

_____

_____

_____

_____

_____

_____

ALL FANTASIES ARE FINE, AND FANTASIES AND REALITY ARE OFTEN NOT THE SAME!

Fantasies that draw our attention are direct links to Shadow. Pleasant or distressing, they reveal our wiring and demand recognition and acceptance.

Let's start with the most basic sex Shadow fantasy facts—all of us have sex fantasies and all fantasies are fine because *fantasy is not reality!*

- Just because you fantasize sex with others doesn't make you unfaithful to your partner! Just because you fantasize extreme or transgressive sexual activities doesn't mean you'd even enjoy them in real life, or need to embody them in the actual world.
- I've known faithful spouses to have promiscuous fantasies, shy people to have dominator fantasies, and dominant men and women to have sexual submission fantasies. It's all fine!

Guy fantasies are often having sex with attractive others. There is wide variety, but, generally, guys have themes, bodies, and scenes that get them off.

- One guy liked two brunettes getting it on.
- Another guy fantasized great times with his wife (the most common male sex fantasy I've encountered).
- One guy only had real sex with women, but fantasy sex with other men.
- Humans are capable of infinite sexual fantasy variations, and it's *mostly* all good.

One caution with sex fantasies—try not to fantasize actual people you relate with. Fantasizing your best friend's wife or husband actually might create distracting attractions with them.

- Fantasizing the man or woman at work might tempt you to cross boundaries.
- Fantasizing sex with your boss might actually lead to a secret affair.

Porn is fine if not used addictively. Know the difference between casual use and compulsive use.

- Casual use is fitting porn/masturbation into a good life and a good sexual relationship with your partner.
- Compulsive use can be daily, extending for hours, interfering with relationships, causing sleep deprivation, or creating obsessive rumination (though, in fairness, many normal young men think about sex almost every five minutes).

Women's fantasies tend to have lots of variation, but usually fall into two categories: scripted and unscripted.

- **Scripted fantasies** have themes and stories, and there are a lot of fun books written about women's scripted sexual fantasies—*My Secret Garden* being one of the most famous. After tens of thousands of therapy sessions and a fair amount of easy-to-read research, it seems to me that women's scripted fantasies involve variations on six major themes:

- **#1: The pretty maiden is the object of another's desire.** I am the adorable sexy embodiment of feminine sexuality who magnetizes my ideal lover. This is an actual genetically-based brain system. Feeling beautiful and desirable elicits physical arousal in many women.

- **#2: I am the sexual victim, the object of humiliation and violence—the ravishment fantasy.** Remember, *fantasy is not reality!* If this fantasy gets you off, you don't want to *really* be raped and humiliated, it is a scene that you control in your fantasy. Again, the ravishment into arousal capacity is an actual genetically-based brain system, almost certainly evolved to protect women being forced to have sex.

- **#3: "I am the wild sexual woman!** I passionately initiate sex which ignites my lover to huge desire for me. Lost in abandoned lust, I consume and overwhelm him with my sexual fire.

- **#4: "I am the dominatrix exerting power, bending my partner to my sexual desires."** Here you dominate, creating an atmosphere of your sexual power controlling, arousing, even humiliating the other.

- **#5: "I am the voyeur, observing others having passionate sex."** You watch them either secretly or openly, becoming more aroused as they progress through their passion.

- **#6: "I am the beloved."** Here you are intimately engaged in lovemaking with a lover of equal power in mutual adoration and passion.

Unscripted fantasies are images or sensations—often fleeting—that can be cued by objects or the environment. In unscripted fantasies there is often a symbolic image focusing on sensual/erotic charge building, building, building . . . and releasing! The image could be a train summiting, a wave breaking, or a flower blossoming.

Fantasies often reflect our coming of age sexuality. Many of us have basically the same sexual fantasies from teenage onward, and all of what is arousing to us constitutes our personal lust map. Our lust map often is set by our teens and then elaborated through life. I've noticed that as I age, I keep adding older women to the women I'm attracted to—one welcome consequence of aging, finding a wider range of women sexually attractive.

EXERCISE 8F
MY SEXUAL FANTASIES

Write down your favorite go-to sexual fantasies, and explore how they fit into the frameworks I've just described. Write down on a scale of 1 to 10 just how embarrassing each one is to reveal to a lover (10 is maximum shame/embarrassment/humiliation, 1 is no-big-deal).

_____

_____

_____

_____

_____

_____

_____

_____

_____

_____

EXERCISE 8G
SHARING SEXUAL FANTASIES

Share these with your lover and ask him or her to do the same with you. If you begin to get turned on, have hot sex! If it begins to turn into a fight, and you can't de-escalate in three to five minutes, talk about it later. If you can't discuss it comfortably at all, take up the conversation with a therapist to help.

_____

_____

_____

_____

_____

_____

_____

_____

_____

_____

_____

_____

9

MARITAL SHADOW

DON'T PRACTICE RELATIONAL DEFENSIVE PATTERNS!

Distress tends to make us feel unsafe and thus elicit defensive states, which in turn tend to threaten our partner and elicit complementary defensive states in him or her. The more often we do this, the more we and our partners co-create enduring relational defensive patterns. As relational defensive patterns continue, we keep activating and practicing them when either of us feels threatened, with each iteration more deeply embedding these destructive habits into our two nervous systems.

The Holy Grail of happy marriages is the *positive habit* of quickly repairing distress back to love. Once both partner's constructive Shadow impulses are simultaneously harnessed to reliably and reflexively seek compassionate understanding and quick repair when in pain, the couple has transformed much of their destructive marital Shadow into constructive marital Shadow.

DESTRUCTIVE INTIMATE BONDING SHADOW OFTEN RESULTS IN LESS SEX AND LESS FUN.

As we explored in the last chapter, sex and fun often require more effort for a couple during intimate bonding. Since sexual urgency fades and defenses amplify during intimate bonding, couples can find themselves having less romance/sex/play (which they miss and *usually* blame the other for) and more conflict (which they *always* blame the other for).

CONSTRUCTIVE AND DESTRUCTIVE SHADOW
IN YOUR MARRIAGE

- Over the last week, what was the moment you felt the most love for your spouse? Write about this in detail.
- Over the last week, what moment did you feel the most distress with your spouse? Write about this in detail.
- Tell your spouse the first story (most love moment) and ask for his or her reactions—then talk about it. Write about this in detail.
- Tell your spouse the second story (most distress) and ask for his or her reactions—then talk about it. Write about this in detail.
- Read everything you've written and look for constructive and destructive Shadow material in you—especially your typical defensive states. Write about this in detail.
- Read everything you've written and look for conflict patterns and love patterns of relating that cause more love or more suffering with you and your spouse. Write about these patterns in detail.
- Share your insights with your spouse and have a discussion. Write about the conversation.

_____

_____

_____

_____

_____

_____

_____

_____

_____

_____

_____

_____

EFFECTIVE REPAIR IS THE CORNERSTONE OF HAPPY MARRIAGES

Conflict comes with the territory of marriage. Effective repair has six major components:

- First, stay positive with your spouse as much as possible so you both generally feel fondness and admiration for one another.
- Second, start a conflict talk gently (especially with tone)—"Honey, I know you've been working hard to remember to do the yard work, but the last couple of weeks I've noticed a lot more football watching and a lot less grass mowing." You'll notice how gentle humor helps a lot. This is not cutting humor where we contemptuously dismiss or use disgusted tones, but engaging humor that makes our spouse smile.
- Third, if your spouse initiates a conflict talk (80% of the time wives initiate such conversations), respond gently—"I don't like how you remind me so

much about house jobs on the weekend, but I know I space out and you have to say something."

- Fourth, both of you need to feel heard and validated for your feelings and desires. Heard and validated sounds something like, "I know the lawn looks terrible and I've slacked off on mowing." "I know I ask you to do a lot of repairs and maintenance around the house during the weekend when you want to relax and have fun."

- Fifth, after you talk, you both feel you've made a little progress on your issue—"I will mow the lawn today." "I will try to not ask you to use all your spare time fixing up the house." Most couples' issues are never fully resolved, but happy couples get better at managing them and making progress.

- Sixth, you both feel affectionate connection at the end. This last is *crucial!* Feeling affectionate connection is not *pretending to feel* affectionate connection, it is actually feeling it and sharing it with your partner with a hug, caress, or heartfelt "I love you!" or "You're wonderful!"

EXERCISE 9B
WRITE ABOUT A SUCCESSFUL REPAIR

Remember a time you and a partner repaired a conflict back to mutual affection. Write about which of the above steps you utilized in your successful repair.

_____

_____

_____

_____

_____

_____

_____

_____

_____

_____

_____

_____

_____

▶ **Affectionate connection sidebar:** _When Becky gets mad at me and we talk about it, I'll ask her a couple of minutes later, "Are you still mad?" If she is, she'll say, "Yes! I'll be over it soon, but I'm not quite there yet!" I usually find this incredibly endearing, because I know the shift to tasty Becky warmth is just a couple of minutes away. This looks easy when we do it, but it is the result of decades of work._

Repair gimmick #1: Break gridlock with open-ended questions about the yearning or dream beneath the resentment.

Repair gimmick #2: Don't trust what you're thinking in defensive states.

Repair gimmick #3: Publicly admit you don't trust what you're thinking right now when feeling angry or defensive.

Repair gimmick #4: Catch yourself putting the relationship on the line (like, "I don't want to be in a marriage where . . ."), or using absolutes, and immediately *apologize.*

USE THE FIVE STARS AS RELATIONSHIP MAINTENANCE TOOLS

In my audio class, *Loving Completely,* I recommend people evaluate potential lovers, themselves, and their spouse by asking five central questions, which I call the Five Stars.

The Five Stars are the five questions:

1. **Is there erotic polarity, a spark of attraction, between my spouse and me?** We have energetic polarities with everyone we encounter, but some polarities have an erotic tingle. If you're a guy, you probably look at your wife sometimes and feel a subtle to huge sexual desire. If you're a woman, you might occasionally think about your husband, "He's sweet," or feel a pleasant (or maybe uncomfortable) awareness of your body as he compliments how hot your new dress is.

2. **Does my spouse maintain his or her physical and psychological health?** They don't have to be buff, they just need to seem interested in staying reasonably healthy and happy, and willing to put regular effort into health. For instance, does he or she eat healthy food, exercise at least moderately, avoid cigarettes and addictions, and ask for and receive help from you and others when having physical or emotional problems?

3. **When we're in conflict, is my spouse able and willing to do what it takes to get back to love?** "Able," asks if he or she has the depth, knowledge, skills, and maturity to deal productively with conflict. "Willing," asks if they can manage their own fears, resentments, and impulses to attack and flee enough to hang in with you in conflict and work back to understanding and affection.

4. **How does my spouse show up as a parent or family member?** We all grew up in some family experience. Does my spouse put him or herself second

when needed by a child? Does he or she relate well and set appropriate boundaries with different family members?

5. **Does my spouse have deep soul's purpose, something larger than themselves, in their life, and does he or she feel appreciation and admiration for what's deeply meaningful—even sacred—to me?** We all have some sense of the sacred, and, after the initial romantic infatuation stage of a relationship burns out, we usually don't want a partner whose *sole reason for being is to be with us.* His or her life must also matter to them separate from us. Also, we need partners who respect and at least somewhat understand what's important or sacred to us. If I take my relationship with God, spirit, or the infinite seriously, I need you to understand and respect how special that is. If you find a deeper connectedness and sense of unity doing yoga, parenting your child, volunteering for youth soccer, or having integrity in your job, you need me to recognize and honor this special area for you.

Using the Five Stars as five dimensions to continually evaluate yourself and your marriage is one way of making sure you don't let important issues slip through the cracks. Remember, marital entropy requires constant attention.

_____

_____

_____

_____

_____

_____

_____

EXERCISE 9C

USING THE FIVE STARS AS A TANTRIC PRACTICE
WITH YOURSELF AND YOUR SPOUSE

- Ask yourself the Five Stars about your spouse and write about it.
- Ask yourself the Five Stars about yourself and write about it.
- Share all this with your spouse and invite him or her to do the same.
- If problems arise that you can't repair after several conversations, get help from a good therapist.
- Every month or so have a Five Star conversation with your spouse to see how you two are doing, and what adjustments you can make now toward fun, love, repair, passion, and growth.

_____

_____

_____

_____

_____

_____

_____

_____

10
PARENTAL SHADOW

We now know:

- That secure attachment styles in parents and children support happiness and optimal development significantly better than insecure attachment styles. Infants and children who get the attunement, space, and attention they need tend to feel solid in the world and confident that parents will be around, safe, and effective. Kids who are neglected, abused, or poorly attuned to tend to struggle—they're more likely to shut down, act out, suffer extreme anxiety, or sink into depression.

- Goodness of fit between parent and child can be improved with conscious parenting. Our kids are born with hard-wired personality characteristics like activity level, rhythmicity, and shyness. Parents who can understand their child's type and adjust accordingly have happier, more successful children.

- Authoritative parenting is better than authoritarian, permissive, or disengaged parenting. Parents in charge, but flexible, fair, and attuned, have healthier children and better marriages than parents who are hostile/controlling, disengaged, or permissive.

- Parents who have a good relationship with each other have healthier kids. A couple taking care of their love helps kids at every age.

- Emotionally coaching attitudes are mostly better for kids than emotionally dismissing attitudes. Viewing emotions as teaching opportunities that need dialogue, labeling of feelings, and problem solving/boundary setting predicts academic and social success, resilience, and a solid sense of self in kids.

- Liberation hierarchies are much better than dominator or chaotic hierarchies. Creating a family structure with compassionate parents firmly in charge, but open to feedback and concerned with care and fairness supports healthy development hugely more than parents who bully, neglect, or can't attune with love.
- Open systems are better than closed systems. Healthy families welcome outside input and enrichment opportunities. They are open to new ideas and new people.
- Growth mindsets are better than fixed mindsets. Effort and progress orientations generate more joy and success than get-the-A/win-the-game-at-all-costs/failure-is-shameful orientations.
- Parents who receive influence to grow are better for kids than parents who think they know it all. Being a superior parent means dedicating yourself to a lifetime of learning how to love your children more effectively.

You see a framework emerging. We want to create secure attachment styles in our kids, and be securely attached to our spouse. We want to support each child's unique temperament. We want to practice authoritative parenting. We want to embody emotional coaching attitudes and behaviors. We want to create liberation hierarchies in our family where things are fair, we share, and we care for each other. We want our families to be open systems rather than closed systems. We want to encourage growth mindsets and not encourage fixed mindsets in both our children and ourselves. We want to keep improving and growing as parents.

What stops us from doing all this all the time?

Shadow.

EXERCISE 10A
PARENTAL SHADOW:

- What was your best moment with you and your mother? Best moment with your father? Write about these moments in detail. What parental characteristics were each of them embodying in these wonderful moments?
- How do you embody these positive parental characteristics? Write how you do.
- What was your worst moment with you and your mother? Your father? Write about these moments in detail. What less-than-optimal parental characteristics were each of them embodying in these painful moments?
- How do you embody these less-than-optimal parental characteristics? Write how in as much detail as possible.
- Write how these moments reflect your constructive and destructive parental Shadow—be alert for the interfaces (similarities, differences, and influences) between who you are now and how your parents were when you were growing up.
- Share all this with your partner. Write about your conversation.
- Share all this with your kids—at any age! There is age-appropriate language for discussing Shadow at every developmental fulcrum—just adjust to your kid's language and thinking abilities and reach to understand his or her interior sense of the world. Interiors are your kid's feelings, beliefs, and subjective experiences. Write about your conversations.
- Read everything you've written and make a list of parental virtues you need to accept and honor in yourself, and then another list of destructive habits you need to improve.
- Share this with someone you love, with an emphasis on how this exercise opens up windows to some of your core constructive and destructive parental Shadow. Write about your conversation.

My kids, Ethan and Zoe, are currently 31 and 28 respectively. I expect to be a better parent next year to them than I am this year. Why? I'm open to new perspectives, I study human thriving and striving, and I know what I believe right now is just my *current best understanding*. Looking back, I'm shocked with how little I knew about infants when Ethan was born and how much more I know about toddlers and children today than when my kids were growing up. I'm appalled at how immature I was in so many ways as Ethan and Zoe progressed through complicated developmental fulcrums. That being said, I did the best I could during those years, and knew far more than my parents' generation (and most of my contemporaries) about almost everything to do with families and childrearing.

On my deathbed I'll hopefully still be working on being a better parent to my children.

> ▶ **Deathbed sidebar:** *Speaking of deathbeds, Australian Bronnie Ware worked as a caregiver for dying people, and asked all of them what they would have changed in their lives—what regrets they had. She found five themes:*
>
> - *I wish I had the courage to live a life true to myself.*
> - *I wished I hadn't worked so hard.*
> - *I wish I had the courage to express my feelings.*
> - *I wish I'd stayed in touch with my friends.*
> - *I wish I'd let myself be happier.*
>
> *All of these in one way or another involve children and family. Even more, how someone embodies each of these has profound effects on his or her children and family. All five regrets reflect qualities these people not only yearned to embody more fully themselves, but often wished to help their children embody more fully.*
>
> *Consider deciding to embody all five starting right now! Live a life true to yourself. Work in a way that supports a balanced life. Express your feelings—with acceptance and caring intent for your experience and others' experience. Stay in touch with the friends and family that bring you joy and love. Consciously recognize each hour of each day that happiness is a choice and you can decide to be happier right now.*
>
> *If you resist improving in these areas you are at a fractal interface between your conscious self and your destructive Shadow—a growth opportunity! Be curious about your resistance and engage in self-reflective dialogue with someone you trust about what might be stopping you and how to make progress in these areas.*

PARENTING TIP: CULTIVATE GROWTH MINDSETS

As I mentioned earlier, growth mindsets are *much* better than fixed mindsets. Effort and progress orientations generate more joy and success than get-the-A/

win-the-game-at-all-costs/failure-is-shameful orientations. Here's an exercise for cultivating growth mindsets.

- Notice when you are more focused on outcomes with your child—like winning, getting the right answer, getting an "A," painting the perfect picture—and when you are more focused on how they are engaged. Are they interested, making efforts, progressing?
- Try to politely acknowledge successes, but visibly enjoy effort, interest, and progress with your kid in everything from chores to schoolwork. Let them know your admiration when they are making efforts and expanding.
- After doing this for a week, ask your spouse how you've been doing as a parent. Others often see us better than we see ourselves, and your spouse will probably report pleasure at your efforts and progress.

GENOGRAMS HELP US UNDERSTAND OUR SPOUSE, OUR CHILDREN, OURSELVES, AND THE FAMILIES WE ALL CAME FROM.

A genogram is getting a big sheet of paper and putting your name in the center, and everyone in your extended family ordered around you in a generational hierarchy with oldest on top. Then you put different lines to brothers, sisters, mothers, fathers, grandmothers, grandfathers, uncles, aunts, cousins, nephews and nieces, spouses, children—everybody—with a solid line meaning a nurturing relationship, dotted line meaning a tenuous or even nonexistent relationship, and a line with horizontal slashes in it a conflicted relationship. Then underneath each name you put a few descriptors that characterize that person—gentle, harsh, alcoholic, unfaithful, faithful, happy, loving, erratic, steady, abusive, nurturing— and especially how they were with you. Monica McGoldrick and Randy Gerson developed the genogram techniques from the ideas of a psychiatrist/researcher named Murray Bowen who studied families around eighty years ago.

Just making a genogram instantly expands your knowledge of yourself and your family. Sharing genograms with your spouse instantly creates insights about your relationship's strengths and vulnerabilities.

EXERCISE 10B
DRAW YOUR GENOGRAM

- Get a big sheet of paper and put your name in the center, and everyone in your extended family ordered around you in a generational hierarchy with oldest on top, youngest children on the bottom. Go at least as far in the past as your grandparents, and at least as far into your extended family as your uncles, aunts, and cousins. You can paste pictures of people—or images, drawings, or symbols—next to their names if you'd like.

- Connect everyone with lines—with a solid line meaning a nurturing relationship, dotted line meaning a tenuous or even mostly nonexistent relationship, and a line with horizontal slashes for a conflicted relationship.

- Underneath each name put a few descriptors that characterize that person—gentle, harsh, alcoholic, faithful, unfaithful, happy, loving, erratic, abusive, nurturing—and especially how they were with you if you had any contact with them.

- Look at everyone and consider that you probably have some capacity to be like many of them, have tendencies similar to some of them, and have destructive and constructive Shadow programming to some extent related with all of them. Write any observations, insights, ideas, and possibilities you discover.

- Many of these people are parents. Look at their styles of parenting—strengths and weaknesses—and consider that you probably share many of those qualities or have developed reactions to things they did. For instance, your father might have been a stoic suck-it-up-and-carry-on type of guy, so you might either be that way yourself, or have resolved to be especially attentive to your child's emotions because your father wasn't particularly attentive to yours. Write about what you discover.

- Share all this with your spouse, and write about your conversation.

- If your kids are at all interested—and they can be at any age—share this material with each of them and write down your conversations, looking for insights on your strengths and weaknesses as a parent and what areas you'd like to focus on growing.

- Share what you've written and discovered so far with your spouse, and pay attention to whether it's a fun conversation or not. If not, try to make it more fun. If you can't make it more fun, ask a therapist to help you two be able to discuss parenting more enjoyably. If parents radically disagree on parenting styles—especially if one is a suck-it-up, avoid-negative-emotions, emotionally dismissing parent, and the other is an emotions-matter, let's-explore-and-learn-from-everything emotionally coaching parent—it predicts divorce with 80% accuracy without therapy, so harmonizing parenting styles is vital for marriages.

_____

_____

_____

_____

_____

_____

_____

_____

_____

_____

_____

_____

_____

_____

_____

_____

_____

_____

_____

▶ **Everyone-has-their-work-to-do sidebar:** *This is why I like to tell couples and families that a healthy family helps everyone develop—Mom, Dad, kids, and even extended family. We all have our current work to do in self-care, emotional regulation, relating better with each other, attuning to others, and ourselves and following our Way. I've found that families with this orientation tend do well.*

GOODNESS OF FIT

Back in 1956, married couple Stella Chess and Alexander Thomas, along with Herbert Birch, started an extensive study of parents and children evaluating nine temperamental qualities in 161 children:

1. Activity level—How much the kid moved around and sought physical motion.
2. Intensity—How emotionally intense the child was about interests and issues.
3. Regularity—How naturally the child created and followed physiological routines like eating, sleeping, and elimination, and psychological routines like family dinners and errands.
4. Sensory threshold—How much sight, sound, touch, taste, and other sensory inputs a child could tolerate comfortably without distress.
5. Approach/withdrawal—The extent to which a child approached or withdrew from different forms of social engagement.
6. Adaptability—How easily or painfully a child adjusted to changes in activity, environment, or relationship.
7. Distractibility—How easily a child drifted from one focus of attention to another.
8. Persistence—How engaged a child stayed with a focus or activity in the face of frustrations or distractions.
9. Mood—The typical affective tone of the child's life—happy, sad, anxious, joyful, social, withdrawn, or angry.

They found 40% of children to be easy—meaning adaptable and easily attuned to social environments, 10% difficult—reactive, rebellious or regularly hard to manage, and 15% slow to warm up—instinctively withdrawn, shy, or cautious. The other 35% demonstrated more complex combinations.

Their work—along with many others—reveals that how well children do depends a lot on how parental personalities and parenting styles fit with each child's temperament. This has been called *goodness of fit*.

- Get a big sheet of paper and create vertical columns for each member of your family—you, your spouse, each child, and other major caregivers of your children. List everyone's name across the top of the sheet.
- On the left side of the paper, make a vertical list of the nine temperamental qualities from the previous page.
- In the boxes that naturally form across the page, rate everyone from 1–10 on each quality. For instance, if you are completely laid back about everything, put down a 1 on intensity. If you are passionate about almost everything, put down a 10 on intensity.
- For each of your children, write what special attention they need for every quality. For instance, if they are very adaptable, they might need acknowledgment for being able to shift modes easily, and perhaps extra interest in what they want as contrasted with what others want from them (a problem with being too adaptable is that you can lose your own agenda adapting to other's desires or demands).
- For you and your spouse, write what special skills you need to practice to help each child. For instance, if you're high intensity and your child has an anxious mood, you might want to practice self-soothing and mindful awareness to be a calmer presence.
- Study your chart and write in your journal about how to create more goodness of fit in your family.
- Share everything with your spouse or someone you love, and talk about how to get support to create more goodness of fit in your parenting.

You now have a goodness of fit roadmap for your family. *You can share this with your kids.* Yes! Let them know how you understand them and yourself, and what you're doing to help everyone thrive and grow. This normalizes a growth mindset for the family—"We're all different. We all have strengths and vulnerabilities. We work to acknowledge and expand our strengths and acknowledge and improve our vulnerabilities. Dad has his, Mom has hers, and each of you kids has yours."

If your child disagrees, change his or her designation to feel more accurate *to him or her.* The purpose is to consider what type of person we are with interest, not to perfectly get every quality right. If you personally find it either super-easy or next-to-impossible to shift your opinions, go back to your 1–10 score on adaptability and see if it predicts your reaction.

Making this chart naturally reveals constructive and destructive parental Shadow in you and your family and it brings the unseen to light. Each day, remind yourself to acknowledge your constructive Shadow strengths and those of your spouse and kids—these are a family reservoir of skills and resources, and we all should know and appreciate our virtues. Each day, remind yourself to acknowledge destructive Shadow tendencies in you and everyone and have regular conversations about how to improve in those areas—normalizing the reality that none of us are perfect, but we can always be growing and learning.

FOUR PARENTING STYLES, AUTHORITATIVE IS BEST

Diana Baumrind is a Berkeley psychologist who identified four major styles of parenting—authoritarian, permissive, uninvolved, and authoritative. Of these four, authoritative consistently had the best child outcomes. Briefly:

- Authoritarian is my way or the highway. Just shut up and do what I say. Authoritarian parenting doesn't work very well. It creates problems in children, because it normalizes bullying in the family. Authoritarian parenting creates dominator hierarchies of parents enforcing rules with fear and violence. Not surprisingly, children from such families are more likely to be physically violent or violently victimized themselves.
- Permissive is, "Sure, do anything you want to do. You want candy, have some candy. You want to break the piano, break the piano." Permissive parenting can turn kids into crazy narcissists.
- Uninvolved is parents communicating on many levels to kids that, "I'm not connected with you because I'm gone, I'm distracted, I don't want to, I'm not interested, or I'm clueless." Uninvolved sucks, but it's not just parents who are responsible—this is a cultural pathology in America

where we work more hours than any other industrialized country. When Mom has to work three jobs and comes home exhausted, she doesn't have much time to connect with the kids—especially if she is among the single moms who are raising over a fifth of the children in this country. When Dad has to put in 55 hours a week to keep up and be successful, there's not much juice left for children. So what happens to kids with uninvolved parents? Usually they're raised by other kids like brothers, sisters, and friends—not good to have kids raising kids. A signature trauma for one adult woman client of Francine Shapiro (the originator of EMDR—eye movement desensitization reprocessing) was when the woman was four she was dropped off at a park with her two-year-old sister whom she was supposed to take care of. It was a signature trauma because she knew that at four she couldn't do an adequate job and something horrible might happen, and the sense of anxious inadequacy continued to haunt her through her development.

• Authoritative is a parent in charge, but fair and kind. An authoritative parent has a moral compass, is attuned to self and child, and enforces rules respectfully, insisting that rules be reasonable and open to dialogue in the family. An authoritative parent will encourage kids to have opinions and even take charge when the kids are coming from mature and caring places. An authoritative parent wants everyone in the family to have power, but takes on the responsibility to maintain fairness and support what's best for both kids and adults.

There's a great book by Lynn McTaggart called *The Bond* where she gathered studies of human cultures and social preferences (McTaggart is a genius at integrating vast amounts of scientific data into accessible and absorbing stories). The consensus of these studies was that when people are given an environment where they can exist comfortably with each other and there's enough food, security, and personal autonomy, they tend to prefer societies that are fair, where they care for each other, and where they share resources. Authoritative parenting tends to produce families—each one a little culture or society—biased to care, be fair, and share.

EXERCISE 10D
WHAT FLAVORS OF PARENT AM I?

Write down incidences of your mother and father being authoritarian, permissive, uninvolved, and authoritative when you were a child.

- Write how you felt about yourself and how you felt about your parent in each instance.
- Write how who you are today might have been influenced by any of these instances or modes of parenting.

Write down incidences of you being authoritarian, permissive, uninvolved, and authoritative—especially with your children.

- Write how you felt about yourself and how you felt about your child in each instance.
- What one aspect of your parenting are you most proud of? Write about it.
- What one aspect of your parenting are you most ashamed of, embarrassed about, or frustrated with? Write about this, and what you would have to do—starting today—to improve in this area.
- Share everything with someone you trust—preferably the person or persons you co-parent with, and especially with your spouse. Write about your conversation.

_____

_____

_____

_____

_____

_____

_____

_____

_____

_____

Please honor your constructive parental Shadow! Your adaptive unconscious holds incredible wisdom about helping each of your children thrive.

Similarly, please honor your destructive parental Shadow! When it intrudes and causes you or your family pain, seek positive influence (from your spouse, friends, therapists, books, audios and videos—there is a wealth of knowledge a click away in the 21st century) and cultivate growth mindsets on gradually turning these vulnerabilities and weaknesses into virtues and strengths.

The following are some indicators to help identify constructive and destructive parental Shadow.

EXERCISE 10E
YOUR CONSTRUCTIVE AND DESTRUCTIVE PARENTAL SHADOW

Discover your constructive and destructive parental Shadow through answering the following questions. Write your responses and share them with people you trust and parent with:

- Attune to yourself and your kid. Easy to attune? Constructive Shadow. Trouble attuning? Destructive Shadow.
- Do you notice when your kid has problems and then respond with warmth and compassion? Constructive Shadow. Don't notice or get easily distressed or frustrated? Destructive Shadow.
- Do you ignore your child's issues, or over-react and make your kid's problems about you? Destructive Shadow.
- Do you have high intimacy and satisfaction in your primary relationship? Does your partner? If so, constructive Shadow. If not, and you're currently addressing the problems, constructive Shadow. If you're unhappy and you're avoiding problems, destructive Shadow.
- Does your child feel safe discussing emotionally painful topics and events with you? If so, constructive Shadow. If not, destructive Shadow.
- Do you feel comfortable discussing emotionally painful topics and events with your child? If so, constructive Shadow. If not, destructive Shadow.
- Do you receive influence on helping your child thrive? If so, constructive Shadow. If not, destructive Shadow.

_____

_____

_____

_____

▶ **Ceremony sidebar:** *We humans are naturally drawn to ceremony, which elevates a moment to spiritual significance either alone or with others. I believe we benefit from ceremonies we create in service of love, growth, and healing. Spiritual seeker and writer Evalyn Underhill suggests that the stages of ceremony for groups include:*

1. *Awakening/initiation—people become aware of the desire to transform, and are drawn to a teaching/spiritually-connecting experience.*
2. *Purification/pacification—the environment is set, the intent is set, the group is called together and unified by the leader.*
3. *Illumination—the message/talk is delivered with the Dharma lesson (some relevant content) for today.*
4. *Dark night—where participants encounter the shadows of doubt, fear, anger, shame, or struggle.*
5. *Unification—where unity is experienced through transcending struggle into transformation.*
6. *Benefit is dedicated to all beings.*

You can organize these stages alone, by you for others, or by others for you. Ceremony strengthens the emotional/spiritual significance of experience and insight. You can organize your own individual and group ceremonies to involve these six stages.

_____

_____

_____

_____

_____

_____

_____

_____

_____

_____

_____

The attunement practices we did in Chapter One can help you develop the self-reflective tools to enable you to expand your awareness of constructive and destructive parental Shadow. You can attune to yourself and others any time, and I encourage you to attune as much as possible. Especially, attuned awareness with acceptance and caring intent of you and your child's inner states and processes sets the stage for thriving children and a happy family.

11
DREAMS, THE ROYAL ROAD TO SHADOW

What are the scariest dream images or sequences you've ever had? Mine have been witches as a child and vampires as a grown up. The first Witch dream I remember happened when I was four or five. *I am running panic-stricken down our Street in Granada Hills, CA, finally making it to the Front Door of our House. Door opens leaving me in a Cooking Pot being held by Leering Witch.*

Notice how I describe the dream in the present tense, as if it is happening now. I also give the proper names of *"Leering Witch, Street, House, Cooking Pot, and Front Door"* to the dream images. I'll keep doing this throughout this chapter. Proper names help us relate *personally,* now in the present tense, to characters and images as individuals. Awarding qualities, landscapes, feelings, colors, and sounds proper names helps us enliven dreams—we want present moment immediacy. In general when we work with dreams, the more vividly we feel them happening right now, the more useful they become.

> ▶ **Trauma sidebar:** *The exceptions to maximizing affective immediacy are trauma memories which can be unbearably emotionally charged, and post-traumatic stress disorder (PTSD) where sufferers are routinely flooded with horrific sensations and images, often in terrifying nightmares. Therapy for these involves reducing the emotional charges into affectively tolerable doses.*

Write your nightmare dream images down with as much sensory detail as possible. Include what you and other characters see, feel, think, and do in whatever dreamscapes they arise from. Do it in the present tense as if it is happening now. Give proper names to each aspect and character of your dream.

_____

_____

_____

_____

_____

_____

_____

_____

_____

_____

_____

_____

_____

_____

_____

_____

_____

Nightmares inevitably involve conflict, usually between a *"Me"* who might or might not be your current body/self, and a frightening *"Other."* Such conflicts often represent or involve actual conflicts we are experiencing, have experienced, or might experience in waking life—either between us and others, and/or between our conscious ego and any of our countless inner selves/voices/attitudes in the past/present/future.

Nightmare caveat: *Some nightmares are rooted in trauma, or are inherently so upsetting that they are literally too scary or too shameful to even consider. If any or all your nightmare images are too uncomfortable for you to deal with alone, it's probably best for you to work on them collaboratively with a therapist.*

LOVELY DREAMS

What are the loveliest, most fun dream images or sequences you've ever had? One of mine is: *I'm soaring like Superman over Beautiful Sea dotted with Lovely Islands. I'm on my way East to something/someplace good—maybe Hawaii.* Write your delightful images down in as much sensory detail as possible.

We'll return to these later.

EXERCISE 11A
BEGIN A DREAM JOURNAL

- Either in this workbook or in a separate journal just for dreams, begin writing your dreams every morning. Write in the first person present tense (I am . . .), and capitalize the names of the figures (Earth, Wings, Bush, Tall Man, etc). Dream images fade fast after waking, so as soon as you wake up write what you remember from the night, in as much sensory detail as possible. If you have no memory of dreams, write what you're feeling and thinking as you wake.
- Notice the emotions associated with your dreams and dream images, and record them also.
- Throughout the day, allow your mind to wander to your dreams, and just stay connected, feeling the feelings and noticing the insights and associations. Record what comes to you in your journal.

The goal of this exercise is more to hang out with dream themes and images rather than interpret or analyze them too much. Interpretation is fine if it doesn't take you away from the lived experience of the dream. For instance, two nights ago I dreamed about surfing, and, uncharacteristically for me, I was catching waves rather than encountering obstacles to getting in the water. A possible interpretation of this dream is that I'm currently actively engaged in meaningful activity rather than feeling blocked—for instance, this book is coming together and feeling much more coherent than it did six months ago. That being said, the image and feeling of pushing myself and my board down onto the face a left breaking wave has a certain alive feel that takes me back to the joy of catching waves (an injury has kept me out of the surf for a long time). The possible symbolism involved is interesting and potentially useful (if I have a chance to go for it in any way I'm more inclined right now to take the risk), but I especially want to keep going back to that stoked moment paddling into the wave. Staying in relationship with the felt experience of the dream is a central principle of all modern forms of dreamwork.

EXERCISE 11B
DREAMS AS AWKWARD CONGLOMERATES

- Look at one of your scary images and list as many components of the scene as possible. Include settings, objects, characters, feelings, themes, thoughts and actions (all with capitalized proper names). Where do these components appear in your current or past life, or potentially in the future? How are they interacting with each other? How does this reflect your current understanding of who you are and what you are about? Write about all this.

- Look at one of your yummy/fun images and list as many components of the scene as possible. Include settings, objects, characters, feelings, themes, thoughts and actions (all with capitalized proper names). Where do these components appear in your current, past, or potential future life? How are they interacting? How does this reflect your current understanding of who you are and what you are about? Write about all this.

_____

_____

_____

_____

_____

_____

_____

_____

FREUD: ASSOCIATING AND INTERPRETING

Freud's approach to dreams emphasized association and interpretation. He would have his patients *associate* on dream images, saying what came to mind as they considered each image or theme. Freud would then weave the associations into an interpretation, essentially a story about the client's life, relationships, problems, or development. In a way, Freudian interpretation of associations involved creating stories from stories, seeking always to clarify understanding and create more coherent life narratives.

Freud changed modernity with his ideas of the unconscious, dreams as symbolic representations of self, and the talking cure. When it comes to dreams, he opened the way for future generations of dreamworkers to journey more deeply into Shadow.

DREAM ASSOCIATIONS AND INTERPRETATIONS:

- Find a comfortable spot, and review what you've written about your scary and yummy dreams.

- One by one take each person, scene, thought, family relationship, emotion, perception, context, and memory, and associate on it. Write whatever comes into your head about what you're considering. For instance, my Witch associations are Woman, Mother, Anger, Dark, Terror, Hunger, Family Home, Courage, Flight, Granada Hills, and Lemon Grove (we lived down the street from a lemon grove). In my flying dream my associations are Light, Power, Joy, Surf, Ease, Blue, White, Ocean, Peace, Islands, and Healing.

- Look over your nightmare associations and look for relationships between dream figures or between your associations and dream figures, and write them down. Write whatever relationships that occur to you. My Witch dream involves relationships with Outside World—I'm running from something scary—as well as relationships with Unsafe Woman and Angry Mother where I'm looking for comfort and finding terror. There are also relationships with Granada Hills House—paradoxically a source of security and terror, and relationships with my two Brothers and Father who are conspicuously absent from the scene. Finally there is relationship with my Young Body—I'm running because I'm too small and weak to defend myself.

- Look over your lovely associations and look for relationships between dream figures, or between your associations and dream figures, and write them down. My flying dream involves relationships with Ocean—magic and vast; with Spirit—I am given transcendent powers; with Joy—freedom of flight and discovery; with Purpose—I know I'm doing something good and meaningful as I fly; and with Blue—my favorite color and the signature color of Krishna, a personal avatar.

- Now read everything you wrote and look for themes, messages, warnings, and insights—essentially your personal interpretations. Pay special attention to any image, idea, or association that has a little burst of reaction in you—an emotional charge, a numbing, or any other reaction. Helpful interpretations almost always involve a shift of emotional charge, a heightening or a numbing. Write everything down in detail.

• Share all that you've written with someone you trust, and talk about what you've discovered and how this is a window into Shadow. Notice how the meanings you've found often morph and shift as you discuss them with another. Notice further how objects and themes often repeat and develop in subsequent dreams you record. As always, be alert for any new ideas or insights, and then write them down.

_____

_____

_____

_____

_____

_____

_____

_____

_____

JUNG

Carl Jung—easily Freud's most famous student—had a much more hopeful view of the unconscious than Freud (who apparently was often quite a depressed guy), as well as Shadow in general, and dreams in particular. Jung thought dreams reflected personal and collective Shadow understanding—power and wisdom that connected us with all peoples in all times. He encouraged clients to extend *association* of dream images into *amplification* where they looked for larger, mythic themes. A Stick picked up off a dreamscape becomes the Sword Excalibur, or Paddle Father used to punish. Angry Woman next door becomes Avenging Fury from Greek Myth, or Raging Mother from childhood.

Jung in many ways is my favorite dream theorist and worker, because of his radical willingness to reconceptualize any framework in response to the needs of an individual client. He said, "[We] should in every case be ready to construct an entire new theory of dreaming." Later in life, Jung expressed dislike for "Jungians" who reified his work and tried to compress clients into theory rather than expand theory in response to clients.

The goal of Jungian psychotherapy is individuation, where increasing harmony of multiple personal and archetypal forces leads to deeper wisdom, compassion, and improved relationships. This is not the homogenization of all our selves and symbols, but their organization into coherent wholes. In this, Jung anticipated subsequent research on adult development where we've discovered that our "Self" can change through adulthood, usually growing wiser and deeper, but sometimes contracting and becoming more rigid and crazy. In other words, constructive and destructive Shadow affects us as we affect it throughout life.

EXERCISE 11D
DREAM AMPLIFICATIONS:

- Find a comfortable spot, and review what you've written about your scary and lovely dreams.
- Choose one image or aspect of your nightmare that has the most emotional intensity. What are the qualities of this intensity? What do you feel in your body as you allow yourself to be absorbed in this image?
- Think of a story, myth, fairy tale, movie, book image or character that epitomizes these qualities. For instance, my Witch can be the Wicked Stepmother Sorceress in Snow White, or Kali the Goddess of destruction. You can also intensify the image into your own archetypal form. My Witch could become a Thunderstorm with dark tentacles reaching out to grab, and hurling lightning bolts to burn. However you amplify, reach for this image or character to feel like a larger, more universal form of your dream aspect.
- Draw, sculpt, or write poetically about this amplified image. Give it as much intensity and juice as possible. Give it a proper name (like Kali, or Sorceress), and find a spot in your house that feels spiritually charged to place what you've created where you can see it daily.
- Choose one image or aspect of your pleasurable dream that has the most emotional intensity. What are the qualities of this intensity? What do you feel in your body as you allow yourself to be absorbed in this image? Think of a story, myth, fairy tale, movie or book image or character that epitomizes these qualities. Reach for an image or character, which feels like a larger, more universal form of your dream aspect. For instance, Ocean in my joyful dream is a character that appears frequently in my dreams, and can exemplify the vast unknown of Shadow—with wonders and monsters concealed in its depths.
- Draw, sculpt, or write poetically about this amplified image. Give it as much intensity and juice as possible. Give it a proper name (like "Ocean"), and find a spot in your house that feels spiritually charged to place it where you can see it daily. This can be the same spot as your nightmare image or a different spot.

- Every day for a week sit for as long as you like in front of your two images/figures/writings while attuning to yourself and attending to whatever thoughts, feelings, images, and memories arise. Write everything down.
- After a week, read everything you wrote and look for themes, messages, warnings, and insights. Pay special attention to any image, idea, or association that has a little burst of reaction in you—an emotional charge, a numbing, or any reaction. Write everything down in detail.
- As you record your dreams, look for these characters returning in the same or different forms. As we relate to dream images and characters, they often change and grow, just as we change and grow over time.
- Share all that you've written with someone you trust, and talk about what you've discovered and how this is a window into Shadow. Write about your conversation.

_____

_____

_____

_____

_____

_____

_____

_____

EMBODIMENT

Inspired by Jung's work, practitioners like James Hillman, Marion Woodman, Jill Mellick and Steve Aizenstat elevate dreams to almost independent status of fellow travelers with self-aware consciousness. They discourage facile interpretation (or often practically any interpretation at all), and encourage an embodied relationship that should be tended and cultivated, looking to uncover dialectics and allow ongoing communion between parts. These approaches advocate elaborate processes and ceremonies to remember, record, process, and relate to dreams and dream images.

Steve Aizenstat, author of *Dream Tending,* advocates two questions to organize all subsequent dream work: Who is visiting now? What's happening here? He goes on to expand dreamwork into every aspect of living and relating, postulating a "World Dream" that encompasses and guides us all. Jill Mellick, author of *The Art of Dreaming,* emphasizes cultural relativism and radical inclusion of all approaches. James Hillman, author of many books on dreams and Shadow including *The Dream and the Underworld,* views dreams as reflections from the "Underworld" that underpin all human experience and culture. He says, "Mythology is the psychology of antiquity. Psychology is the mythology of modernity."

Jung and the depth psychology movement he inspired were among the first psychotherapists to harness the power of dreams, imagination, and storytelling for psychological growth, healing, and understanding. This work anticipated the humanistic psychology movement of the 60s and 70s which has since morphed into the Positive Psychology and Transpersonal Psychology of today, where enhancing health and supporting development have become more central to psychotherapy than diagnosing and curing psychopathology.

Fritz Perls, the founder of Gestalt Therapy in the 1960s, believed every part of a dream represented a part of the Self. Trained in psychoanalysis, he was impatient with the slow pace of psychoanalytic work. The classical psychoanalyst cultivates a neutral relationship with the patient until the patient projects old figures (father, mother, teacher, abuser, savior) onto the therapist (called positive and negative transference), thus making the underlying conflicts available to be worked on in the therapeutic relationship. Fritz found he could accelerate projection using dreams and other life events in conjunction with imaginative processes. He pioneered the now famous empty chair technique of alternately talking to dream fragments, then embodying them to respond. These dialogues often progress from initial resistance, to conflict, to reconciliation and integration. For instance, you may dream of a locked door in a house. Your therapist asks you to have a dialogue with Door, switching identities from you to Door:

You: "Let me in Door!"

Therapist: "Now be Door responding."

You: "I don't want to be Door!" People often initially resist Gestalt dialogues—sometimes because it feels awkward, and sometimes because it can be scary to personalize and relate with dream images and characters.

Therapist: "Try it," and you agree, imagining yourself to be Door talking to you.

Door: "I'm closed and locked! Stay away! Don't try to come in!"

Therapist: "Be you and respond to Door. Include how you feel."

You: "Let me in, Door! I can handle whatever is in the room. This is frustrating!"

Door: "I'm just trying to protect you. I'm afraid you'll be hurt."

You: "I like it that you want to protect me, but I want to go in."

Door: "I trust you more now. I'm opening."

In your imagination you cross the threshold into the room and discover what's inside, with Door as your ally.

EXERCISE 11E
DREAM ANIMATIONS

- Find a comfortable spot, and review what you've written about the images we've been working with, including the associations and amplifications we did in previous exercises.

- Have a Gestalt dialogue with a scary amplified image/character. You can use two empty chairs and move from one to the other, you can write the dialogue in your dream journal, or you can move back and forth from you to the image/character as you sit in the same place. Make sure each time you speak you express how you feel (what emotion or sensation you're having) as you or the image/character you're embodying. If the dialogue feels unsafe, bring in a third character that you trust—a wise dream figure, Buddha, Christ, or your imagined perfect therapist. Give them a voice and let them weigh in.

- Do this each day for at least three days. Write about your experiences in your dream journal. Especially attend to how you and the figure change and how your relationship changes over the series of dialogues. If this feels useful, continue it until the figure eventually becomes an ally, perhaps a personal ambassador to destructive Shadow.

- Have a Gestalt dialogue with a lovely amplified image/character. You can use two empty chairs and move from one to the other. You can also write the dialogue in your dream journal, or you can imagine being yourself and the image/character alternately as you sit in the same place. Make sure each time you express how you feel (what emotion or sensation you're having) as you or the image/character you are embodying. Do this each day for at least three days. Write about your experiences in your dream journal. Especially attend to how you and the figure change and how your relationship with the figure changes over the series of dialogues.

- Now read everything you wrote and look for themes, messages, warnings, and insights. Pay special attention to any image, idea, or association that has a little burst of reaction in you—an emotional charge, a numbing, or any reaction. Write everything down in detail.

- Share all that you've written with someone you trust, and talk about what you've discovered and how this might be a window into Shadow.

EXERCISE 11F
HARNESSING DREAMS TO SOLVE PROBLEMS

- During the day, be alert for any problems you might have unsolved, or questions you might have unanswered. Write them down when you think of them.
- Shortly before sleep, read what you've written and cultivate any sense of curiosity or hunger for a solution you have associated with these questions and problems.
- Upon waking write down whatever dream fragments, feelings, or insights that you remember or that occur to you. These don't have to be directly related to your question or problem, just whatever you remember, imagine, or think. Let this material play in your consciousness throughout the day, and look for how it might relate to your questions.
- Do this daily for a week, and then review everything you've written.
- Share any experiences, insights, creative flashes, or solutions you might have experienced with someone you trust. Be aware of how the conversation goes and write about it.

12
VIOLENCE SHADOW

WE NEED TO BE AT PEACE WITH OUR VIOLENT SELVES

Much as we might dislike violence in ourselves and others, it is a disaster to deny, ignore, or dissociate from violence. Our sense of personal power necessitates relationships with our violent selves—the parts of us which, for whatever reasons, want to damage others, ourselves, or the world unnecessarily. Men and women disconnected from, or conflicted with, Shadow violence feel weaker and shallower to themselves and others than people with robust and pro-social relationships with their violent selves. Violence Shadow is important because our power as humans and our coherence as conscious beings needs us to tap the wellsprings of power that our violence provides.

FINDING YOUR VIOLENT SHADOW

Remember the last time you were angry with another person—really ticked off—with as much detail as possible. Now, answer the following questions in this workbook:

- What did this person do to piss me off?
- At the time, what was my most primitive impulse? As I recall my mind and body while angry, what impulses arise? Do I want to attack physically? Attack emotionally? Turn and walk away? Do I want to angrily surrender to the aggressor, as in, "F%&* you! Have it your own way!"?
- How do I feel at this moment remembering these impulses? Entertained? Ashamed? Guilty? Righteous indignation?
- What did I do at the time? Attack? Walk away? Lie? Surrender? Engage in cooperative dialogue? And how did the event eventually resolve?
- How do I feel right now about how I handled the situation? Good? Bad? Satisfied? Ashamed?
- Now consider this "me" who got angry and had the primitive impulses as a character—a person whom you can give a name to, like Angry Self, Violent Self, or Chester. What does your Chester look like? Sound like? Feel like? Create a picture, sculpture, or collage that represents this figure. What does this character want from you at this moment as you do this exercise?
- Have an empty chair dialogue with this figure like we did with the dream images in the last chapter. Write what you and your Chester say, and how each one of you feels each time you talk. Continue the dialogue until you feel at least an increased shared understanding between the two of you.
- Continue the dialogue daily for five days. On the sixth day review everything you've written and look for what has been revealed, what has changed, and what has stayed the same. Write about these observations.
- Share everything you've written with someone you trust and write about the conversation.

We co-create universes all the time, blending what's happening and what we are experiencing into *a personal story of now*—where I can be a victim, a bully, a Warrior, a Man of Wisdom, or clueless, depending on my capacities and choices.

Creating present moment universes reaching for compassion and depth of consciousness guides us to use our instincts to violence for good. We can observe the threat, the anger, and the destructive impulses arising from Shadow, and dialyze them with conscious compassion until we discover the way through that supports health and love *for everyone.* Even if we have to set a boundary, give our child a time-out, confront our boss or employee, repel a mugger in alleyway, or criticize our husband or wife, the actions are less violent and more in service of love.

EXERCISE 12B
VIOLENT SELF AS ALLY

Go back to the angry figure from our previous exercise—you know, "Violent Self, Angry Self, or Chester."

- Think of a conflict you're currently having with anyone, and have a dialogue with your Chester about the situation. Keep going back and forth until you feel you have a just and respectful course of action. Write about this.
- Try this exercise around any conflict or irritating situation over the next week—talk about it with your Chester. Write about your experiences.
- Share everything you've written with someone you trust, and ask him or her what he or she sees as the optimal integration of you and your Chester. Write about the conversation.

_____

_____

_____

_____

_____

_____

_____

_____

_____

_____

_____

_____

_____

_____

_____

_____

_____

RADICAL HONESTY

Most people hungry for the deepest truths about themselves and others are open to new input and loving influence. Seeking understandings validated by science, self-reflection, shared intimacy, or social research tends to provide the clearest views, the best relationships, and optimal life directions.

Such clarity requires dedication to Truth as we know it. Yes, there can be exceptions that protect people's feelings and self-esteem, but such exceptions are more rare than most of us think.

EXERCISE 12C
TWO DAYS OF RADICAL HONESTY

Decide to be fully resolved for 48 hours to completely live your principles, and tell no lies. Tell other people you're doing it—don't keep it a secret. Each day, write in your journal what you are feeling, wanting, thinking, judging, and then share it with someone you trust.

_____

_____

_____

_____

_____

_____

_____

_____

_____

_____

_____

_____

_____

LEARN HOW TO TAKE THE HIT

Self-awareness of destructive Shadow often requires we take the hit of shame emotions (regret, guilt, embarrassment, self-doubt, disgust, mortification, or humiliation) when we acknowledge the destructive thought, impulse, or act, before we can feel the relief of resolving to do right in the present moment and behave better in the future.

Part of doing right is recognizing that an impulse or fantasy is not an act, that the past can't be changed, and that I always have a choice to listen to my wiser, more loving self right now, and act on what Wise Self tells me.

EXERCISE 12D
TAKE THE HIT AND ADJUST TO COMPASSION

Remember the last time you were mean or unkind—emotionally or physically violent—to another person. Write about this in detail. Include:

- Details of what happened.
- How you felt about yourself and the other at the time.
- How you feel about yourself and the other right now.

Remember the last time you were mean or unkind—emotionally or physically violent—to yourself. Write in your workbook:

- Details of what happened.
- How you felt about yourself at the time.
- How you feel about yourself right now, remembering the episode.

Now go back to each example and write your most compassionate understanding of you and the others in the scenes. Include:

- Contexts—what might have motivated the behaviors.
- Defensive states that you and the other might have been in.
- What positives you forgot about others and yourself—things like, "She always does her best to not hurt people," or "I was trying to solve the problem and got sidetracked by frustration."
- Write how understanding this situation can help you think, feel, and act better in the future.
- As you do this, how do you feel about yourself? Do you feel like a kinder and better person? Do you feel wiser and more mature? Less ashamed? Write about this.
- Share everything you've written with someone you trust.

All forms of violence radically affect both constructive and destructive Shadow. Whether we're the perpetrator or the victim, implicit Shadow material arises demanding our attention.

EXERCISE 12E
INTEGRATING OUR VIOLENCE

Review all your responses to the exercises in this chapter, and ask yourself, "What have I learned about my Shadow violence?" Write your answer in as much detail as possible.

- Now ask yourself, "What have I learned about Shadow violence in general?" and then write your answer in as much detail as possible.

- Finally, ask yourself, "What am I likely to notice in the future that I didn't notice previously?" and then, "How am I likely to be different in the future than I have been previously?" Write your answers in as much detail as possible.

- Share everything with someone you trust, and write about your conversation. Notice if this talk leads you to deeper intimacy or more separation from this person, and, if possible, share this with him or her.

_____

_____

_____

_____

_____

_____

_____

13

CREATIVITY—SHADOW DEMANDING EXPRESSION

Creation needs perception. Perceiving new things helps us create new things, and we can *create* new perceptual systems. Am I fulfilled in my relationship? Is my partner? Am I in a defensive state or state of healthy response? Am I speaking or thinking primarily from my deepest, most authentic self? Am I speaking or thinking from pride? Ego? Instinct gratification? Altruism? Interdependence or codependence? Am I being true to my deepest purpose, or betraying my deepest purpose? Learning how to consistently answer these questions grows us new perceptual systems. As we develop them our capacities to generate love, wisdom, and art amplify and expand, because these new perceptions push the fractal boundaries between what we know and don't know into greater complexity. This is especially true if we can harness our default mode networks, executive attention networks, salience networks, and mindwandering networks with focused intent and action, in service of principle, and driven by resolve—always in relationships with others and the many parts of ourselves.

All of this book's exercises encourage self-awareness and new sense organs—creative new perceptual capacities. All the exercises encourage new insights and opportunities for growth and love. One reason you're probably reading this book is that, as we grow, we increasingly seek out like-minded others to share our manifestations and service, because like attracts like, creativity attracts creativity, and love attracts love.

Write about the last time you felt the pleasure of making something. A poem, meal, garment, picture, party, date, collage, song, dance—anything you did/ made/composed/thought/imagined/said that gave you pleasure.

- What motivated you to create? Was it momentary discomfort? For example, "I'm hungry. I need to create a meal," or, "I'm bored. I need to create entertainment." Was it an emotional surge that required expression—like a poem, song, painting, or conversation? Was it a direction from (or obligation to) another person—like homework, a request, a work assignment, or an inspirational idea? Write in detail about how the motivation felt, and how your feelings changed as you became engaged in the creative process.

- Did you experience flow states during your task—some kind of effortless, timeless pleasure feeling in sync with forces seemingly larger than yourself?

- If you did have periods of flow, write about how they felt and how you transitioned into them and out of them. Did focused intent and action lead you into flow? Did minor interruptions jerk you out of flow?

- How did you feel right after you accomplished your goal? Satisfaction? Dissatisfaction? Loss? Pleasure? Narcissistic delight? Remember that healthy narcissism is feeling appropriately great about yourself, while unhealthy narcissism dismisses or demeans others. Some studies suggest that experiential thinkers who value perception, intuition, and emotional surges in their creative work have more anxiety and self-doubt after finishing a project than rational thinkers who prefer logical analysis of problems. Write about how you felt in your body and what thoughts accompanied the feelings right after you accomplished your goal.

- Now look at your daily routine with new eyes—alert for every moment that requires your creative manifestation. What is your reaction to this view of yourself as constant creator? How does it feel and what do you think? Write about this, recognizing that your journal entries are all creative acts.

MINDFUL MANIFESTATION AND CREATIVITY

There are many systems that have been developed to support creativity—all effective. Mostly they simply teach us to yearn, discern, and act. "Yearn" is attending to what draws us. "Discern" is evaluating and clarifying what goals, perspectives, and actions serve our deepest purpose and values. "Act" is where the rubber hits the road and we *do* something in service of our goals.

It's six o'clock PM and you're hungry. You yearn for food. You discern that you have some chicken and lettuce in the refrigerator. You make a Chinese Chicken Salad. You have manifested dinner. What most proponents of mindful manifestation maintain is that the main difference between manifesting dinner and manifesting a million dollars (or a painting of a sunset, or tap dancing) is that we are certain we can make dinner and are willing to keep at it until dinner is ready, while we tend to be uncertain about whether we can manifest the million, paint the sunset, or learn to tap, and tend to be discouraged when we encounter problems along the way.

COMMON ELEMENTS OF MINDFUL MANIFESTATION

We all unconsciously create all day long, but we also *consciously* create, where we deliberately choose a goal and move toward it—*mindful manifestation*. There are almost as many mindful manifestation systems as there are teachers. Even though they sometimes don't use the terms "Creativity" or "Manifestation," people from every walk of life, discipline, and profession have methods for setting goals and realizing them. The systems I've encountered tend to have five elements in common:

1. Self-reflective centering while establishing goals.
2. Visualization and embodiment of goals into images and language, often using present tense ("I am . . .") affirmations while cultivating gratitude for the goal *already realized* (I can imagine the joy of generating a pill that cures Alzheimer's, a book that changes a culture, or a movie that captures a zeitgeist).

3. Ceremonies of daily activities often involving regular productivity, contemplative practice, networking, generating teams, resting and recuperating, and welcoming input from many sources.

4. Inevitable problems that are best met as interesting challenges and growth opportunities rather than as humiliating rationales for avoidance and desertion of project and self.

5. Personal transformations, unexpected life consequences, and subjective experiences of being in harmony with vast spiritual/energetic beings or forces.

_____

_____

_____

_____

_____

_____

_____

_____

_____

_____

EXERCISE 13B
WRITE A PERSONAL MANIFESTATION STORY

- Remember a time that you wanted something and then created it or otherwise made it happen.
- Write a story of how it happened, with you as the central character, in as much detail as possible.
- Go back over the story and underline or highlight all the parts related to yearning with one color of marker, all the parts related to discerning with another color, and all the parts related to acting with a third color.
- When you're done, put the pages on the floor in front of you in sequence and observe what you feel, think, and imagine as you see your personal manifestation story spread out and highlighted before you.

_____

_____

_____

_____

_____

_____

_____

EXERCISE 13C
MINDFUL MANIFESTATION

What is a current goal of yours? A new car? More fun with your children, husband, or wife? Lose ten pounds? Make a movie about dog training? A trip to Bali? Learning how to make pasta? Write down your goal in as much detail as possible.

- Find a comfortable spot and attune to yourself, breathing deeply in your belly and attending to what you sense, feel, think, judge, and want with acceptance and caring intent. As you feel stable in your attunement, send your attention to your goal.
- Visualize your goal already accomplished and describe it in your workbook in present tense terms—"I am driving my new car to the beach," "I see the delight in my son's eyes as we walk into Disneyland together," "I feel intense love and desire for my husband as I kiss him and relax into his embrace."
- Make a list of specific actions you could do daily for the next month to move toward your goal, with as much specific detail (what, where, when, and how many) as possible. Include asking others for help and networking to support your project.
- Anticipate at least four problems that will arise and what you'll need to do specifically to resolve them toward accomplishing your goal. Write the problems and solutions.
- Resolve to follow your plan for a month and be open to insights and personal transformations along the way.
- Enact your plan and record daily experiences and progress.
- After a month, review everything and write about how you feel differently or the same about yourself or your goal than when you started.
- Share everything you've done with someone you trust.

DAYDREAMS AND CREATIVITY

Daydreams come in three general categories.

- *Positive constructive* where we are happily solving problems or lost in fantasy.
- *Guilty dysphoric* where we generate memories, images, or fantasies involving shame, anger, sadness, fear, confusion, disgust, or anxiety.
- *Poor-attention-control/disjointed* where we can't focus and are easily distracted.

Those positive constructive daydreams are the heart and soul of human creativity and constructive Shadow. They pull us into what's *personally* important, yummy, beautiful, and good, giving us flashes of emotions, insights, impulses, stories, and images that can be harnessed into creative acts. Positive constructive daydreams generate creative fantasy, problem-solving, and happy reverie—all gifts of self-aware consciousness and central to understanding, processing, and moving through the world. Positive constructive daydreams serve creativity in multiple ways, and are generally constructive Shadow happily informing our moment to moment life.

DAYDREAMS

Pay attention to what kinds of daydreams you have today and tomorrow and write about them in your workbook.

- If they are positive constructive, relax into them with interest.
- If they are guilty dysphoric, ask yourself, "What positive constructive thoughts can I have about this topic?" and pay attention to what feelings, thoughts, images, or ideas emerge—especially about you.
- If your daydreams are poor attention control/distracted, kindly direct yourself back to the task at hand.
- Consider an ongoing practice of cultivating positive constructive daydreams and recording insights/ideas/images, etc., that emerge.

_____

_____

_____

_____

_____

_____

_____

_____

_____

_____

_____

_____

_____

_____

_____

_____

_____

_____

WHAT ARE SOME OTHER METHODS TO MAXIMIZE CREATIVITY?

We've established that humans create constantly, do it both consciously and unconsciously, and that we can cultivate downloads, but what are some other ways to boost creative capacities and maximize what we've already got? Science and the wisdom traditions have yielded some obvious and not-so-obvious answers to these questions. Let's visit some of them, and feel free to give yourself assignments to practice any that appeal to you.

- Set aside a regular time and spot for creative activities and then relax into whatever comes during that time. Early morning is often good since we often are solving problems in our dreams. Between four and five o'clock PM is also good because our conscious mind—centered in our left hemisphere—is fatigued and thus our non-conscious, Shadow-driven right hemisphere has fewer obstructions to sending us creative insights. In general, be curious and open when the left hemisphere is fatigued or cut off (as in intoxication, taking a shower, or absorbed in a non-demanding task).
- Engage in creative activities regularly! Nothing supports creative output more than the activity of creation. You're more likely to paint a masterpiece if you do a hundred paintings than if you do three paintings.
- Embrace influence from wise others! Share your work with people you trust and admire and ask for direction in making it better. In this sense, dialectics with others where we are authentically reaching for new perspectives are priceless intersubjective fountains of creative thoughts, ideas, and actions.
- Write or record dreams, insights, and images down as they arise. Think about them, look at them later during your dedicated creative times, share them with others, and look for patterns to arise.
- Rub different knowledge areas or disciplines against each other, creating fractal boundaries where novelty can arise. My friend Ken Wilber—author of numerous books and the main originator of Integral theory—once told me he'd read to a PhD level in twenty-three different disciplines (the guy reads a lot!). It's no wonder he came up with Integral meta-theory (a theory about theories) that unifies the empirical with the phenomenological, and adds valuable new perspectives to any approach put through the Integral lens.

A central feature of Integral psychology is how worldview affects the universe we live in. Let's look at worldviews and creativity.

ELLIS PAUL TORRANCE AND THE BEYONDER CHECKLIST

Ellis P. Torrance knew something about creativity—at least if one measure is *volume*. His work includes 1,871 publications: 88 books; 256 parts of books or cooperative volumes; 408 journal articles; 538 reports, manuals, tests, etc.; 162 articles in popular journals or magazines; 355 conference papers; and 64 forewords or prefaces—what a prolific guy! He also was a good guy. By most accounts Torrance was a warm friendly companion, colleague, and husband. He lived from 1917 to 2003 and was obsessed with creativity in all its forms. His test of creativity—the Torrance Test—is a foundation instrument in the field.

Torrance was the one who predicted that creativity and IQ would be correlated at low but not at high scores, known as the threshold hypothesis, and this was borne out by subsequent research. He found other variables associated with the highest levels of creative output, the sum total of which he called "The Beyonder Checklist." These qualities are all learnable and include:

- Love of work
- Sense of mission
- Deep thinking
- Tolerance for mistakes
- Well-roundedness
- Feeling comfortable as a minority of one

He measured these qualities in a number of teens and young adults and followed them for fifty years (*think about doing an experiment for fifty years! You have to have a lot of patience and passion to keep one study going for five decades!*). Sure enough, the subjects high on the Beyonder Checklist had the most creative output in their lives.

The *big variable*—the one measure with the most predictive power—was falling in love with your dream, with your image of the future.

This last was also validated by Catherine Cox who studied the creative output of people from 1450 to 1850 and found that passion plus persistence predicted creative output more than simple genius.

EXERCISE 13E
FIND YOUR PASSION AND PERSISTENCE

In your journal write down each of the following sentence stems at least five times, and as you repeat them to yourself generate different answers that you write down.

- The most important work of my life is . . .
- One situation where I have the most willpower is . . .
- The creative activity that gives me the most pleasure is . . .
- Someone whose work and mission I admire is . . .
- I yearn for . . .
- I'm jealous of . . .
- I desire . . .
- I envy . . .
- I despise . . .
- I would be satisfied if . . .
- I would be happy if . . .
- I love . . .
- Read your answers every day for a week, and then write what you've discovered about your passion and persistence. Clarify these goals as specifically as possible by writing, drawing, or gathering images or literature reflecting them already accomplished. Put key messages and images that support your missions on your mirrors, your refrigerator, or your dashboard where you can see them daily, and cultivate gratitude for them already accomplished.
- Share everything with someone you trust. Write about your conversation.

_____

_____

_____

_____

_____

_____

_____

_____

_____

_____

_____

_____

_____

_____

_____

_____

———————————————————————

———————————————————————

———————————————————————

———————————————————————

———————————————————————

———————————————————————

———————————————————————

———————————————————————

———————————————————————

———————————————————————

WORLDVIEW AND CREATIVITY

In the last century, Claire Graves noticed how individuals, groups, and cultures tended to lean toward these different worldviews, and his work has informed such developmental luminaries as Ken Wilber, Don Beck, Chris Cowan, Robert Kegan, and Susanne Cook-Greuter. Everybody agrees that individuals and couples grow through these stages in an include-and-transcend manner, and often are more informed by one motivational system than another.

What are *your* relationships with your different selves and their creative outputs?

EXERCISE 13F
MEET SOME OF YOUR DIFFERENT SELVES

Get a big sheet of paper and list in a column down the left side egocentric, conformist, rational, pluralistic, and Integral. Now let's get to know these parts of you better!

- Think about your egocentric self, the part of you concerned with your pleasure, safety, personal power, and comfort. Pick an image, character, or dream person that most personifies this part of you and write about him, her, or it in detail opposite "Egocentric" on your sheet. Give him or her a name if you'd like. I imagine Keith happily catching a wave on a sunny day, or lying on my couch with a glass of wine watching my favorite Ultimate Fighter in a championship fight. When you are done, imagine that character/image/dream figure sitting opposite you and look into his or her eyes and say what you're feeling and wanting. Especially ask that figure what he or she wants you to create for him/her/it. Then change places and be that character looking you in the eyes and answering. Go back and forth like this at least several times, and write what you say, think, feel, judge, want, and imagine as you do this.

- Think about your conformist self, the part of you concerned with fitting in and being accepted by people with your beliefs. Pick an image, character, or dream person that most personifies this part of you and write about him/her/it in detail opposite "Conformist" on your sheet. Give him or her a name if you'd like. I imagine Keith out to dinner with my favorite interpersonal neurobiologists and colleagues (as well as my wife and two kids) and we're enjoying each other's stories and ideas—feeling comfortably part of the same belief systems. When you are done, imagine that character/image/dream figure sitting opposite you and look into his or her eyes and say what you're feeling and wanting. Especially ask that figure what it wants you to create for him/her/it. Then change places and be that character looking you in the eyes and answering. Go back and forth like this at least several times, and write what you say, think, feel, judge, want, and imagine as you do this.

- Think about your rational self, the part of you concerned with success, recognition, and being consistent with the way the world really works. Pick an image, character, or dream person that most personifies this part of you and write about him, her, or it in detail opposite "Rational" on your sheet. Give him or her a name if you'd like. I imagine Keith in a $2000 suit presenting to rollicking laughter and thundering applause at UCLA's yearly Lifespan Learning conference, while *Shadow Light: Illuminations at the Edge of Darkness* is hitting the bestseller lists. When you are done, imagine that character/image/dream figure sitting opposite you and look into his or her eyes and say what you're feeling and wanting. Especially ask that figure what it wants you to create for him/her/it. Then change places and be that character looking you in the eyes and answering. Go back and forth like this at least several times, and write what you say, think, feel, judge, want, and imagine as you do this.

- Think about your pluralistic self, the part of you that feels that everyone's opinions and feelings count, and that everyone should be treated equally well. Pick an image, character, or dream person that most personifies this part of you, and write about him, her, or it in detail opposite "Pluralistic" on your sheet. Give him or her a name if you'd like. I imagine me making a case before Congress for universal healthcare and massive material and social support for mothers, fathers, and children from conception onward. When you are done, imagine that character/image/dream figure sitting opposite you and look into his or her eyes and say what you're feeling and wanting. Especially ask that figure what it wants you to create for him/her/it. Then change places and be that character looking you in the eyes and answering. Go back and forth like this at least several times, and write what you say, think, feel, judge, want, and imagine as you do this.

- Think about your Integral self, the part of you that appreciates and accepts all the above characters and motivation systems, and can mostly discern the healthy and unhealthy aspects of each. Pick an image, character, or dream person that most personifies this part of you, and write about him, her, or it in detail opposite "Integral" on your sheet. Give him or her a name if you'd like. I imagine me in a Shrink and Pundit dialogue with my good friend Jeff Salzman, trying to help everyone live, love, and work more joyfully and successfully, while knowing that everyone enacts a different universe requiring different insights and missions. When you are done, imagine that character/image/dream figure sitting opposite you and look into his or her eyes and say what you're feeling and wanting. Especially ask that figure what it wants you to create for him/her/it. Then change places and be that character looking you in the eyes and answering. Go back and forth like this at least several times, and write what you say, think, feel, judge, want, and imagine as you do this.

- Talk with each of these (going back and forth looking into each other's eyes at least two or three times) every day for the next month. As the days pass, notice how you become more marginally aware of all of them at different times. You are developing new sense organs to monitor these parts of you, as well as new powers to listen, respond, and self-regulate. You are also learning how to discern the healthy and unhealthy manifestations of each worldview's constructive and destructive Shadow.

- Cultivate relationships with these five of your most central selves, all of whom want you to create, but who all have different emphases of motivations. As these relationships become a background hum to your life, you are amplifying the fractal interfaces between your conscious self and adaptive unconscious. From these interfaces will arise insights, images, desires, feelings, and stories.

- The more you have a felt appreciation for the strengths and weaknesses of all these selves, the more your Integral self becomes the central voice, with a felt appreciation for the strengths and weaknesses of all points of view and dramatically less fear of the world, including of your own death.

Multiple points of view interacting, cross-validating, and mutually enriching, have been associated with amplified creativity in all disciplines, and *you contain all these voices*—they all send Shadow messages to you each day. These worldviews are *always informing you* one way or another.

Do these exercises and you accelerate and clarify new material arising from constructive and destructive Shadow into your conscious awareness—you expand your boundaries of understanding and amplify your creative output and grow your creative Shadow self.

_____

_____

_____

_____

_____

_____

_____

_____

_____

_____

_____

14
SPIRITUAL SHADOW

Nervous systems resist shame by building hardwired shifts to different states (defensive states), still painful, but feeling more self-protective than shame. This begins in infancy and accelerates until we can finally take charge of the process and turn defenses into growth. We've explored defensive states individually and in relationships in previous chapters. Let's look at them developmentally, as most of them began with our nervous systems programming defensive states to avoid *pain*.

What do these defensive avoidance states look like? Let's visit four-year-old Karen and her Mom, Kate. As I enumerate a few of little Karen's possible defenses, imaging how they might play out in adulthood if she *never* learns how to perceive them and integrate them into healthy responses to the present moment.

Momma Kate leaves Karen alone in the living room with new crayons—big mistake, Kate! When she notices five minutes of suspicious silence, she gets an uneasy feeling and walks in to see Karen happily drawing on the walls, eliciting an angry, "Oh no! Stop that right now!" from Kate. Let's look at a few paths their nervous systems might take to deal with the anger and shame:

- **Healthy reactions:** Karen looks down in shame, "I'm sorry Mommy." She begins to cry, getting that she screwed up and feeling bad about it. Kate takes a deep breath, resists her impulse to keep yelling and blaming, and says with the kindest tone she can muster, "You know you're not supposed to draw on the walls!" Karen says, "Yes Mommy, I won't do it anymore." Kate hugs her and says briskly, "All right, let's clean everything up!"

- **Reaction formation**. Karen looks down in shame, and then recoils to energizing rage. She throws down her crayons and starts a full-on temper tantrum. This leads to a power struggle and an unsatisfying time-out while pissed off Kate cleans the wall alone.
- **Projection**. Karen says, "Tommy (her younger brother) did it!"
- **Denial**. "I didn't do anything."
- **Rationalization**. "Look at the pretty colors I put on the wall."
- **Scapegoating**. Karen turns to her long-suffering puppy and screams, "Go away!" as it cowers down.
- **Retroflection**. Karen says, "I'm sorry Mommy. I'm a bad girl and you should spank me." Jumping on the "I'm bad, punish me," bandwagon is a strategy many diligent children develop to try to control the pain of shame.

We all have programming like this, ready to pop out if we feel shame, anxiety, or distress. Most such defenses are distortions, which block us from sensing and feeling Soul.

DEVELOPMENTAL DEFENSES

When you were little, a grade schooler, or in high school, what were your go-to defenses to deal with disapproval? Did you project and blame others for doing what you were caught doing? Did you deny? Did you rationalize destructive behavior with elaborate excuses and explanations? Did you attack the person disapproving? Did you attack yourself? Write about this with special attention on:

- How connected or alone you felt when in a defensive state.
- How willing you were to give up the state when confronted (or soothed) by yourself or another.
- How much you still practice these particular maneuvers, with which people, and how it feels when you do it.
- What the impact these defensive habits have had on your life.
- How close to or disconnected from Spirit you have felt when in the grips of such states.
- When you're done share everything you've written with someone you trust.

_____

_____

_____

_____

_____

_____

_____

_____

_____

_____

_____

_____

_____

Self-aware consciousness comes with a price. This is the deeper meaning of the Prometheus myth, where the cost of fire was eternal suffering, but the light and creative powers were worth it.

SPIRITUALITY AND STATES TRAINING

Many contemplative practices, religious ceremonies, psychotherapeutic systems, and personal development approaches involve learning how to instantiate particular states of consciousness, like presence, loving kindness, dialed-in mindfulness, unity with pure emptiness, or non-dual experiences of simultaneous absolute emptiness and absolute fullness. Countless studies have shown numerous positive effects from such practices including lowered blood pressure, increased heart rate variability, better affect regulation, accelerated growth in progressive worldviews, and actual changes in the size and wiring of critical brain areas.

Most modern seekers develop their own combinations of states practices that they find helpful, and I personally benefit from a number of practices I do daily. I've found one extended meditation to be particularly beneficial and I'm going to share it with you.

ONE OF MY CORE PRACTICES—9 CHAKRA MEDITATION

Raising the Kundalini energy is a central tantric practice found in many Eastern yogas. Cultivating centered, peaceful, or transcendent states defines most contemplative traditions. One of my foundation practices is raising Kundalini energy while practicing twenty-eight different transcendent states.

Each time you enter a state of consciousness, the neural networks associated with it become more mylinated and hardwired. Particularly in my work I wanted my constructive Shadow to have ready access to a wide variety of transcendent states to show up when needed while I'm teaching, writing, or doing psychotherapy. I also want it to become easier and more habitual to discern and surrender to constructive Shadow in all its forms. I developed this meditation to practice transcendent states the way a pianist plays scales.

This particular practice is informed by the Wilber/Combs Lattice (from Allan Combs and Ken Wilber), a charting of the ascending chakras as they manifest in gross (concrete materialistic), subtle (imaginative and energetic), causal (pure emptiness), and nondual (everything at once). Lighting up each chakra, starting with the root chakra and moving up nine chakras is one of my favorite daily routines.

This practice combines the Integral state concepts of gross, subtle, causal, and nondual with the process of raising the Kundalini. Through nine chakras this yields 28 distinct states, since causal—pure emptiness—is the same for each chakra. Doing the practice is very much like a musician practicing scales, it strengthens each state as well as abilities to shift states, and I've found it enormously useful as well as personally transformative. I'll define some terms and then show you how it's done. Feel free to take any or all of these steps in combinations that feel right to you and to include them in your personal spiritual activities.

GROSS, SUBTLE, CAUSAL, NONDUAL

- **Gross** is "real world" concrete manifestation. It is the first level of concrete experience.
- **Subtle** is all the variations of this level, including imaginative, subtle energies and spiritual variations, in this universe and beyond.
- **Causal** is pure formlessness—emptiness, no-thingness—which is the same in all chakras.
- **Nondual** is the all-at-onceness of self/world/everything-as-that-chakra as one taste or experience.

THE PRACTICE

- **Sitting meditation:** This practice can be done sitting in stillness, with eyes open or shut.
- **Moving meditation:** This practice can be done exercising, walking, or any other safe activity (your attention gets divided so you need to use relatively safe, easy, repetitive activities). I do it sitting, lying in bed, swimming, and walking in nature.

Choose which states to practice: It's not necessary to do all 9 chakras, or even all 4 states in any chakra. Feel what's most comfortable and transformative for you and practice those states. Each one of them is a particular flavor of bliss. I will describe my experiences, but yours will be your own flavors.

Choose how long you inhabit any given state: You can hold any one of the states for seconds, minutes, or longer. Teaching yourself to shift from one to the other strengthens your salience network, divergent thinking, and access to the other world.

1ST CHAKRA: THE ROOT CHAKRA/PHYSICAL EMBODIED REALITY—ASSOCIATED WITH THE BASE OF THE SPINE

- **Gross:** I feel my physical being connected with everything in gross reality such as gravity, electromagnetism, atoms, and molecules, etc., all the way up to the universe expanding at a constantly accelerating rate (physicists are still puzzling about what causes *that*). I relax into expanding universe.

- **Subtle:** I am aware of all the forms—from cosmic strings, to tiny drops of water, to galaxies—as unique expressions of holarchies, connected and separate. I usually feel a sense of devotional awe for the mysteries of subatomic to transgalactic manifestation.

- **Causal:** Anchored in admiration and adoration for all forms, I feel for pure emptiness from which everything is constantly arising. This is often a fade-into-black dissolution experience that is pleasurable, but requires some practice if you're moving around. I've occasionally walked into cars or collided with another swimmer if I don't make sure I stay oriented to the physical world.

- **Nondual:** From pure emptiness, I sense the miracle of the universe continuous arising—flowing from emptiness into fullness, into one taste of all physical reality.

2ND CHAKRA: LIFE IN ALL ITS FORMS—ASSOCIATED WITH THE PELVIC/ABDOMINAL AREA

- **Gross:** I feel fields of all life, including mine, connecting in the fields of life that encompass earth and beyond. Inherent in everything and me are the sensual drives to survive, thrive, be intimate, procreate, and create. I feel the sweet pleasures of life with a little thrill up and down energy channels from above my forehead through my root chakra and legs into the earth.

- **Subtle:** I see each blade of grass, tree, microorganism, animal, person, as a miracle of life with genetic roots back to our first single-celled ancestors. This usually involves floods of love for each plant, bird, animal, insect, and microorganism I consider.

- **Causal:** Anchored in admiration and adoration for all life, I relax into pure emptiness from which everything is constantly arising.

- **Nondual:** From pure emptiness, I feel the unity of all life, past/present/future, as one joyful song/motion/taste/sensation. I'm intensely aware of my sensual interfaces with everything, even as I experience all life as joyful suchness.

3RD CHAKRA: THE POWER CENTER—ASSOCIATED WITH THE SOLAR PLEXUS

- **Gross:** I feel myself connected to all the powers of the universe, from supernovas to a single virus, to a sub-atomic particle that might become another Big Bang, to any human capacity for choice, action, thought, and influence. The sense is relaxing into dancing with unimaginably powerful forces, adding my infinitesimal powers to the constantly moving/evolving energies of the universe and beyond.
- **Subtle:** I feel profound respect and admiration for all the powers, and sense the increasing consciousness and choice as power ascends the evolutionary scales into individual capacities for violence and compassion, unwise influence and wise influence. I feel all my own powers existing in this energetic matrix.
- **Causal:** Anchored in respect and resolute acceptance of all powers everywhere, I feel for pure emptiness from which everything is constantly arising.
- **Nondual:** From pure emptiness I feel one with the power of the universe, channeled through me as Warrior, willing to die for principle, one with both the void and infinite torrents and shapes of energy.

4TH CHAKRA: THE HEART CHAKRA OF ALL LOVE—ASSOCIATED WITH THE HEART AREA

- **Gross:** I feel my love contributing outward to all the fields of love that encompass everything in loving embrace.
- **Subtle:** I am aware of how all holarchies are expressions of love, of matter reaching to affiliate with matter in coherence and increasing harmony

with the whole, dramatically amplifying love up the evolutionary ladder to the fields of love that each person, couple, family, and tribe have for one another, into Universal Love. A line from a Jim Steinman song, *Heaven Can Wait,* sometimes comes me at this point, "And all the Gods come down here just to sing for me."

- **Causal:** Anchored in love for all the fields everywhere, I feel for pure emptiness from which all love is constantly arising.
- **Nondual:** The universe is all love all the time and I am that love, serve that love, and surrender to that love. Big Heart. Divine Love.

5TH CHAKRA: EXPRESSION AND COMMUNICATION— ASSOCIATED WITH THE THROAT

- **Gross:** I feel my voice/being/transmissions as part of the universe as language in the broadest sense. Subatomic particles communicating with other subatomic particles, to all the conversations, books/videos/verbal/non-verbal expressions of matter and life. Terrence McKenna once said that the universe is language. I feel immersed in endless communication.
- **Subtle:** I feel each expression as a miracle, from atoms informing atoms, to sap flowing through the oak tree, to all human exchanges, both trivial and profound. I am part of a cornucopia of communication, all self-organizing and fluid.
- **Causal:** Riding the torrents of all the communications—the universe as language—I feel for pure emptiness from which communication is constantly arising.
- **Nondual:** From emptiness I feel the Kosmic "Om" from before the Big Bang to after the end of the universe, with all my communications, contributions, and transmissions being multiple channels where I give and receive simultaneously, constantly transforming others as others transform me—***all at once.*** I get senses of fields projecting endlessly in all directions from my throat chakra.

6TH CHAKRA: THOUGHT—CENTERED BEHIND THE THIRD EYE

- **Gross:** I feel my thought fields interpenetrating with all the thought fields, all the beliefs and thoughts that coexist in the universe—especially dense around life and superdense around self-aware humans.
- **Subtle:** I feel how thoughts influence and ultimately harmonize/alter/cross-validate each other with infinite variations. These thoughts are fields connecting and mutually influencing, and I relax into their interpenetrating clouds, feeling peaceful and intensely *aware*.
- **Causal:** Anchored in connection to thought fields everywhere, I feel for pure emptiness from which consciousness is constantly arising.
- **Nondual:** Pure presence flows from emptiness in the 6th chakra. I rest in pure presence, and often think about Eckhart Tolle saying how he loves sitting in presence.

7TH CHAKRA: ALL CREATION—ASSOCIATED WITH THE CROWN AROUND THE TOP OF THE HEAD

- **Gross:** I feel myself relaxing into the evolutionary force for greater complexity that permeates every particle and field in the universe. Pure creation is the field from which evolution arises. To me it's a subtle bubbly energy that permeates everything and sparkles with all colors.
- **Subtle:** Evolutionary forms are manifest in matter, life, and rising into humanity waking to the Universe Dream. I feel awe at eight billion humans, each generating a unique cosmos, all connected and spilling over into each other, iterating back into the collective as novelty expands into the unknown and unformed. Behind is the past, constantly reevaluated and reunderstood as we surf the crest of the evolutionary wave toward countless imagined futures.
- **Causal:** Surrendered to the interpenetrating evolutionary fields of consciousness, I feel for pure emptiness from which creation is constantly arising.

- **Nondual:** I am Big Mind, created and creator, timeless and timefull. I feel mature, *big*, centered, and intimately entwined with creation.

8TH CHAKRA: FIELDS OF CONSCIOUSNESS—THE UNIVERSE AS FIELDS UNDULATING INTO DENSER AND LESS DENSE LEVELS OF ORGANIZATION—FROM QUARKS TO YOU

- **Gross:** I am aware of everything as fields, popping in and out of existence, self-organizing to greater coherence at every level.
- **Subtle:** I feel how all the fields are constantly relating and feel myself as multileveled coherent fields. The Keith consciousness (a blob of fields) blends with people and nature fields, and with time and space fields. This is enormously peaceful, because my sense of self shifts to a subtle conglomeration of fields embedded in fields—pure witness consciousness of my fields of awareness interfacing with all other fields.
- **Causal:** Surrendered to the self-organizing fields that comprise everything, I feel for pure emptiness from which they constantly arise.
- **Nondual:** Everything is simply lively awareness, and I remember Daniel P. Brown talking in awe of feeling everything as lively awareness in a lecture he gave on Mahamudra Buddhism in Terry Patten's *Beyond Awakening* webseries.

9TH CHAKRA: NONLOCAL, TRANSTEMPORAL—I EXPERIENCE NO SPECIFIC PLACE FOR THIS CHAKRA, BUT THE AREAS ABOVE MY HEAD FEEL VERY ALIVE

- **Gross:** I click into no-time, no-space, all-at-onceness, and everything seems like one taste, touch, note, event.
- **Subtle:** Every moment of every object that's ever existed and will exist, all at once, each object having an epic story from the Big Bang to the end of the universe, connected to everything else all the time. Indescribable sense all-at-onceness.

- **Causal:** From the overwhelming sense of all-at-onceness it is relaxing to drop into pure emptiness.
- **Nondual:** Avatars start inhabiting my body, usually beginning with Krishna as a man or youth. Avalokiteśvara in her female form and other archetypal figures occasionally show up. I feel their delight in my precious human body and their desire to manifest and serve through me.

As I suggested earlier, this practice like any other used to expand understanding and compassion supports liberation and the integration of conscious self into constructive Shadow.

> **Be careful sidebar:** *One cautionary note is that these states are blissful and intoxicating. If we use these (or any other) practices to avoid necessary pains, they become a form of spiritual bypass.*

How do we know the difference between healthy use and spiritual bypass? Stay open, curious, available to caring influence, and willing to change perspectives, opinions, and practices as you find better alternatives. Find guides, teachers, and friends you resonate with, and receive influence from them.

When you're curious about (often entertained by) destructive spiritual Shadow, your own and other's spiritual bypasses, and grateful for constructive spiritual Shadow you are probably doing just fine.

Struggling with all these issues is the Shadow of Spirituality.

FINAL EXERCISE

Write a letter to your future self who happens to pick up this workbook. Begin it with something like, "Dear Future Self . . ."

- Remind Future Self of the material from Shadow Light you especially want him or her to remember and keep embodying. Include ideas, insights, stories, or practices you found most useful or exciting.
- Show the letter to someone you love.

APPENDIX FOR THERAPISTS

Shadow Light and *The Shadow Light Workbook* were written for the educated lay public, but they're also designed to help therapists work with Shadow from a variety of Integrally informed perspectives.

As an Integrally informed therapist I want to help my clients heal, grow, love well, and access what feels best and most relevant at each moment from all quadrants, levels, lines, states, and types (AQUAL). I also want to encourage my clients to understand themselves from AQUAL perspectives as much as possible, knowing this accelerates their vertical development—it helps them grow up.

The Integral model is a meta-theory (it organizes many theories within a comprehensive framework) that understands the world from a variety of central perspectives. The core constructs of Integral are Quadrants, Levels, Lines, States, and Types:

- **Quadrants**—Individual subjective phenomenological perspectives, individual objective empirical perspectives, shared intersubjective experiences, and interobjective standards, data, and communications.
- **Developmental lines and levels**—Different development progressions on capacities and abilities like cognition, interpersonal relating, moral development, or skills training.
- **Structure stages**—Humans grow through progressive worldviews from egocentric, to conformist/traditional, to rational/modern, to pluralistic/post-modern, to Integral, and beyond.

- **States of consciousness**—Defensive states, contemplative states, states of healthy response to the present moment, states training, and the relationships between cultivating states and developing traits are all part of a larger states understanding.
- **Types of people**—Different types of babies, men, women, archetypal identifications, and the endless variations of human personalities exist in every culture and have huge impacts on all aspects of our lives.

Deep understanding of these dimensions can change everything in the way you understand yourself and the universe—it can help you wake up and grow up. As I mentioned in the introduction, to dive more deeply into the Integral meta-theory read any of Ken Wilber's books—and to therapists I especially recommend *Integral Psychology, Integral Spirituality,* and the *Kosmic Consciousness* audio class.

SHADOW LIGHT OFFERS A THEORETICAL/PRACTICAL UNDERSTANDING WITH ROOM FOR MANY SHADOW APPROACHES

I have always been a psychotherapist, first and foremost. I'm biased to perspectives and practices that are most accessible to my clients and most effective in helping them be healthy and true to their values—horizontal health in the Integral framework—as well as helping them grow to more mature perspectives and deeper consciousness—vertical health in the Integral framework. Like Carl Jung who once said he created a new theory with each new client, I'm always working toward more fundamental and practical understandings in general and in specific for different types of people at different stages of development, in different relationships, with different strengths and vulnerabilities, at different moments.

Part of what most attracted me to Ken Wilber's Integral epistemology originally was his idea that any perspective I have right now is just the best perspective I have right now, and more beautiful, good, and true perspectives exist and can arrive at any time.

I encourage you to blend your ideas and techniques with the ones you enjoy most from *Shadow Light* and *The Shadow Light Workbook* and pay attention to how your natural healing style expands—just paying attention generally accelerates development.

SHADOW AND PSYCHOTHERAPY

The basic premise of *Shadow light,* is that we each possess a vast information processing network operating out of our conscious awareness—*Shadow*—which constantly communicates constructive and destructive messages via impulses, images, stories, memories, and emotions. These communications can be avoided, ignored, elaborated on, or processed for better or worse by our conscious selves, and how well we do this determines much of who we are and how quickly and well our unconscious Shadow selves grow. Growing our Shadow means literally growing and strengthening our unconscious adaptive information processing selves so they work more harmoniously with our most mature values and conscious awareness.

Ask your favorite therapist about Shadow work and they'll almost certainly respond with some version of psychotherapy being an intimate alliance with clients helping their inner selves grow to support more equanimity and love and less violence everywhere. If you're a therapist, this probably rings true for you.

Shadow work in *Shadow Light* and *The Shadow Light Workbook* involves recognizing and embracing constructive Shadow influences, and dialysizing destructive influences ("Cleaning up" in Integral language).

My belief is that this fundamental and practical understanding makes Shadow material and Shadow work way easier for therapists and clients, and provides plenty of room for other Shadow conceptualizations and practices. In my opinion, Freud's libido theory, Jung's ideas about archetypes and collective unconscious, Allan Schore's work on the adaptive unconscious, all the colorful and intricate books on Shadow and Shadow work, and Ken Wilber's understanding of Shadow being "I" that has been either repressed, dissociated from, or otherwise turned into "You" or "It," being turned back into "Me," all fit with this.

This understanding can help clinicians choose which combinations of Shadow approaches to use in their work, knowing that all involve a common purpose of encouraging constructive Shadow and healing destructive Shadow.

INTEGRAL THEORY PERMEATES *SHADOW LIGHT*

Integrally informed therapists will recognize the Integral meta-theory permeating this book.

Ultimately all healers develop natural healing styles, and I think superior psychotherapy training helps students discern and enhance their natural healing styles. The beauty of a meta-theory like Integral is that you can put any theory/system into it—like cognitive behavioral therapy, Gestalt Therapy, Internal Family Systems Therapy, Affect Regulation, neurofeedback, EMDR, Interpersonal neurobiology, etc., and the meta-theory expands and amplifies your approach. Expanding and amplifying your natural healing style is a central feature of the path of the healer.

SPEAKING *FROM* INTEGRAL MORE THAN *ABOUT* INTEGRAL

Even though Integral understanding is central to my life and work, it presents a variety of problems transmitting it to others. I've had difficulties with this, as have many other teachers and therapists. For instance, out of thirty sessions I might have in a week, I speak specifically *about* Integral constructs in around ten of them on average, and speak *from* Integral in all of them.

Just as with my clients, I decided in writing *Shadow Light* to speak *from* Integral much more than speaking *about* Integral.

INTEGRAL UNDERSTANDING IS PSYCHOACTIVE, BUT FIRST YOU NEED TO *GET IT*

One reason I chose to speak *from* Integral more that *about* Integral is that I've often had difficulty inspiring my clients and students with the transformative nature of Integral understanding.

Those who get it light up as I and all of my fellow Integrally informed friends and colleagues have. Integral is a psychoactive system—partly because it is a *meta-theory* which organizes and connects all theories—that literally changes how you view yourself and the world *once you get it*.

I've observed that those who don't get it at best listen politely, and at worst get impatient with the conversation.

In *Shadow Light,* and *The Shadow Light Workbook* my approach has been to present material I've found priceless speaking *from* AQAL with strategic references *to* AQUAL, in the hopes that readers might become excited and intrigued enough to decide to dig deeper into the Integral meta-theory—that they might be more interested in *getting it*.

One obvious problem with this approach is that by not teaching the AQAL language up front, and then referring back to it again and again as I explore different content areas, the books are potentially less enjoyable to Integrally informed readers who like speaking the Integral language.

I tried this approach of first explaining Integral and then presenting my ideas through Integral frameworks with my books on Integrally informed psychotherapy, *Waking Up* and *Sessions* and had mixed success. Those who read the books often said they enjoyed them, but others reported turning away from the AQUAL constructs *before they fully understood them.*

This problem of "If you get it you're transformed," vs, "If you don't get it the system doesn't excite you," has fascinated many of us in the Integral movement and has resulted in endless conversations and experiments in transmitting Integral as a meta-theoretical scaffolding that can help guide us into the current awakening happening all over the world.

Shadow Light doesn't try to teach the Integral epistemology outright, but instead presents Integrally informed perspectives and practices that have excited me and helped hundreds of my clients.

STEALTH AGENDA

So, as I mentioned in the Introduction, I have a stealth agenda in these books! I'd like to intrigue readers with glimpses of, and references to, the Integral meta-theory while speaking from it on every page. My hope is that cumulatively this might predispose non-Integrally-informed readers to go deep enough into the Integral meta-theory to *want to get it.*

How successful this stealth strategy will be remains to be seen, but the creative advance into novelty requires we take risks and try new approaches.

INTEGRALLY INFORMED PSYCHOTHERAPY

I've conducted over fifty-five thousand therapy sessions (and counting) in my career. With each person, couple, or family I work with I am constantly looking for opportunities to help them become more healthy and true to their values while being alert for opportunities to help them experience more mature and compassionate visions of themselves and the world. I suspect all Integrally informed therapists would say the same in their own words.

Shadow Light is designed to address the ongoing challenge of integrating conscious awareness with constantly emerging unconscious material, both constructive and destructive. If you are a therapist, I suspect you've found formulations and practices in these pages which will help you enormously with your healing work—they've certainly helped me!

Even more, the material in *Shadow Light,* and *The Shadow Light Workbook* has supported my growth as a healer and a person, and I hope it does the same for you.

Lifelong development and commitment to embodying your healing values is what Integrally informed psychotherapy is all about!

Author Bio

D^r. Keith Witt is a Licensed Psychologist, teacher, and author who has lived and worked in Santa Barbara, CA, since 1973.

Dr. Witt is the founder of The School of Love, at www.drkeithwitt.com, where he offers his *School of Love Lecture Series*, blogs, *Therapist in the Wild* webseries,

and Integral Conversations audios and videos on health/love/relationship/sexuality/spirituality/development/psychotherapy related topics.

Keith's work has explored Integrally Informed Psychotherapy, intimacy, human development, spirituality, and sexuality yielding seven books (*Integral Mindfulness, Waking Up, Sessions, The Attuned Family, The Gift of Shame, Shadow Light*, and *Shadow Light Journal*), three TEDx talks, and lectures and classes which he has taught across the U.S.

Waking Up and its companion volume, *Sessions*, are two of the first texts on Integrally Informed Psychotherapy. His popular audio class, Loving Completely, is offered through *Integral Life*. Keith has conducted over sixty thousand therapy sessions, led many groups, and has been a contributor to *Integral Life* and the *Journal of Integral Theory and Practice*.

In presentations around the country—including Integral Life's *What's Next*, Integral Theories Conferences, and his ongoing series, *The Shrink and the Pundit* with Jeff Salzman—Keith has explored love, intra and interpersonal relationships, and development from multiple perspectives, weaving neuroscience, Integral theory, wisdom traditions, and numerous forms of psychotherapy into a coherent cosmology of love and development.

Dr. Witt contact info:
website: drkeithwitt.com
email: keith@drkeithwitt.com
Office phone: 805-569-1102

Mailing address:
P.O. Box 3097
Santa Barbara, California 93130